SCHÜLER-LERNKRIMI
ENGLISCH

Tatort Schließfach

Woods Delaney

Compact Verlag

Bisher sind in dieser Reihe erschienen:

- Compact Schüler-Lernkrimi Englisch, Französisch, Spanisch, Latein I und II
- Compact Schüler-Lernkrimi Deutsch: Grammatik, Aufsatz
- Compact Schüler-Lernkrimi Mathematik, Physik

In der Reihe Lernkrimi sind erschienen:

- Compact Lernkrimi Englisch, Französisch, Italienisch, Spanisch: Grundwortschatz, Aufbauwortschatz, Grammatik, Konversation
- Compact Lernkrimi Englisch GB/US: Grammatik, Konversation
- Compact Lernkrimi Business English: Wortschatz, Konversation
- Compact Lernkrimi Deutsch: Grundwortschatz, Grammatik

In der Reihe Lernthriller sind erschienen:

- Compact Lernthriller Englisch: Grundwortschatz, Aufbauwortschatz, Grammatik, Konversation

In der Reihe Lernstory Mystery sind erschienen:

- Compact Lernstory Mystery Englisch: Grundwortschatz, Aufbauwortschatz

In der Reihe Lernkrimi History sind erschienen:

- Compact Lernkrimi English History: Grundwortschatz, Aufbauwortschatz, Grammatik, Konversation

In der Reihe Hörbuch Lernkrimi sind erschienen:

- Compact Hörbuch Lernkrimi Englisch: Geübte Anfänger, Fortgeschrittene

Weitere Titel sind in Vorbereitung.

Chefredaktion: Dr. Angela Sendlinger
Redaktion: Christine Tuth
Fachredaktion: Fiona Cain
Produktion: Wolfram Friedrich
Illustrationen: Sonja Heller
Titelillustration: Karl Knospe
Typographischer Entwurf: Maria Seidel
Umschlaggestaltung: Inga Koch

ISBN: 978-3-8174-7611-4
7276113

Besuchen Sie uns im Internet: www.compactverlag.de

Vorwort

Mit dem neuen, spannenden Compact Schüler-Lernkrimi könnt ihr eure Englischkenntnisse auf schnelle und einfache Weise vertiefen, auffrischen und überprüfen.

Die Freunde Sarah, Kevin, Simon und Julia erleichtern das Sprachtraining mit Action und Humor. Die vier und ihre spannenden Erlebnisse in den Schulferien stehen im Mittelpunkt einer zusammenhängenden Story.

Der Krimi wird auf jeder Seite durch abwechslungsreiche und kurzweilige Übungen ergänzt, die das Lernen unterhaltsam und spannend machen.

Prüfe dein Englisch in Lückentexten, Zuordnungs- und Übersetzungsaufgaben, in Buchstabenspielen und Kreuzworträtseln!

Dieses Sprachtraining im handlichen Format bietet mit 75 Übungen die ideale Trainingsmöglichkeit für zwischendurch. Schreibe die Lösungen einfach ins Buch!

Die richtigen Antworten sind in einem eigenen Lösungsteil zusammengefasst. Im Anhang steht außerdem ein Glossar, in dem die schwierigsten Wörter übersetzt sind. Diese sind im Text kursiv markiert.

Und nun kann die Spannung beginnen ...

Viel Spaß und Erfolg!

Inhalt

Story

Endlich Ferien! Sarah, Kevin, Simon und Julia sind glücklich: bei strahlendem Sonnenschein können sie nun sechs herrliche Wochen ihre Freizeit genießen. Der beste Treffpunkt dafür ist natürlich das Freibad.
Doch plötzlich verschwinden auf rätselhafte Weise Dinge aus den Schließfächern. Als auch noch Kevins nagelneuer CD-Player gestohlen wird, ist er außer sich. Die Polizei nimmt die Anzeige auf, kann aber keine Verdächtigen ermitteln. So versucht Kevin auf eigene Faust, die Täter zu finden. Wer ist für die Diebstähle verantwortlich? Und wie werden die Schließfächer ausgeraubt, obwohl die Türen nie aufgebrochen sind? Für Kevin steht fest, wer die Diebe sind. Auf abenteuerliche Weise verfolgt er ihre Spur, um sie zu überführen. Aber seine Freunde haben einen ganz anderen Verdacht.
Werden sie es schaffen, die wahren Diebe zu stellen?

Crime Scene: Locker Room

"School is finally over. I thought the summer holidays would never come," said Simon.

"I didn't think I would survive another day of school," said Sarah, "not with the *beady eyes* of Mr Jones watching my every move." Sarah liked most of the teachers, but Mr Jones, the school headmaster, was not a favourite. "He's really *creepy* sometimes."

"He's all right," said Simon. "I'm sure he's as happy about the summer holidays as we are."

The two were standing directly in front of the school. It was the end of July, and there was no more school until the beginning of September.

Übung 1: Unterstreiche die zehn Wörter, die falsch geschrieben sind, und verbessere sie!

They felt free but didn't know what to do with their fredom.

Simon was *handsome* and shy, and though Sarah was not exactly pritty, she was interesting and *outgoing*. Usually her hair was pink, but sometimes she *dyed* it green or some other strange colour. Her noise ring had been a bit of a shock at first. There was no written school rule that said you couldn't get your nose pierced, but everyone knew that you couldn't. And then Sarah had got her nose pierced. In the meantime many boys and girls were whering such rings – and getting their eyebrows, their lips, their tongues pierced as well. Sarah was moar than a hair colour or a piercing, though. She had personality, *charm* – "*that certain something*," as thay say in Hollywood. They might have made a good cupple, but whenever they were together Simon could think of nothing werth talking about. Every thought that came into his head seemed stuppid, so he hated the idea of being alone with Sarah. She had no idea how to read Simon's silences. Was he uninterested, boared or was he simply comfortable with the silence?

"Hey, Simon, what are you doing?" Kevin, Simon's best friend, was calling to him from across a busy street. Over his clothes he was wearing *kneepads* and *elbow pads* and he was holding his skateboard under his arm. Kevin was a skateboard freak. There were only two places he didn't bring his skateboard – in the shower and in bed. His skateboard was a bit *battered*, but Kevin loved it.

ÜBUNG 2 !

Übung 2: Setze die Verben ins Simple Past!

"I don't know," Simon (1. to answer) __________, looking at Sarah helplessly. "And you?"

"I've got to go home," Kevin (2. to say) __________. "I promised my mum I'd help her with the *spring cleaning*."

"A bit late for that, isn't it?"

"Yeah. She wants to throw a lot of *stuff* away, and I've got to make sure she doesn't throw anything of mine away. I've got lots of CDs and cassettes she'd just love to *get rid of*."

"If the weather's nice tomorrow, we could meet at the pool," Simon (3. to suggest) __________.

"I'll see if I can get away. I do need to work on my *suntan*." Kevin (4. to set) __________ his skateboard down, put his *headphones* on and pressed the play button on his CD player, got on the skateboard and (5. to skate) __________ away down the pavement and out of sight.

Simon and Sarah (6. to look) __________ at each other. The silence between them (7. to be) __________ *uncomfortable* for both and becoming *unbearable*. Sarah finally broke the silence.

"So, do you *fancy* going to a music shop and having a look around?"

"Um, yes, er, no, I mean, um, why not?"

Sarah smiled at him, but there was a little bitterness in her smile.

"You don't have to come, Simon. You can do what you like."

"No, I do want to come, I do. It's just that …"

"What?"

"Nothing."

"I feel *like* I'm *pulling teeth*."

"No, it's not that. Sometimes I just can't tell what I'm in the *mood* for. But looking through CDs would be just the thing."

"Let's go, then," Sarah said, walking away from the school.
Simon followed her. After looking through CDs for more than an hour, they sat at a café and had a cup of tea.
"I don't think we have the same taste in music," Simon said.
"I never thought we did. But that doesn't really matter, does it? I mean you can introduce me to things that you like and I can tell you about things I like. We can bring new ideas into our band." They were members of a band called The Sneakers. Simon played guitar, Sarah played drums and Kevin played bass. Other friends played saxophone and keyboards. They were taking the summer off, though, since they would all be going away with their parents on holiday at different times.
"Well, I must be off," Sarah said, "let's pay."
Outside the café, Sarah said, "Bye, Simon."
"Bye, Sarah." They looked at each other a moment. They both wanted to get away but were not sure if they had said goodbye in an *appropriate* way. "Maybe we'll see each other at the pool."
"Pools are not exactly my thing," Sarah said. "They aren't punk rock." Her nose ring sparkled in the sunlight.
Neither am I, thought Simon, but he said, "I suppose not. But I'll be spending a lot of time there just the same."
"Maybe I'll see you there then."
"Kevin will be there too."
"Bye," Sarah said and walked away.

ÜBUNG 3 !

Übung 3: Setze das richtige Fragewort ein!

1. ____________ are you doing tomorrow?

2. ____________ did you go last night?

3. ____________ did you turn the television off?

4. __________ is your favourite actress?

5. __________ old is your father?

6. __________ is the name of the French president?

7. __________ movie do you want to watch – this one or that one?

8. __________ has the best CD collection?

9. __________ do you want to meet tomorrow? After lunch?

The next day was beautiful. Usually it rains on the first day of the summer holidays – which is the price one has to pay for nearly six *glorious* weeks of no school. No one in the city expected such a beautiful day. The *lifeguards* were ready, though. They knew the city pool was going to be *overcrowded*. There had been few bathers the past few weeks, mainly tourists and people on holiday. Now, with the start of the school holidays, the summer would really begin at last.

Simon got to the pool around 11 am. He paid the *entry fee* to the *lifeguard* at the entrance, changed in the *locker room* and then walked out to the poolside. He put his towel and a shirt across two white plastic *deckchairs* to save them before walking up to the pool and looking at all the people. There were little boys running around and screaming, pushing each other into the pool, jumping off the *diving boards* and going feet-first into the water. There were girls who joined the boys in their rough games and girls who swam around together like little schools of laughing fish. It was chaos. Simon was a good swimmer, but with so many people in the water there would be no swimming.

! ÜBUNG 4

Übung 4: Vervollständige die Sätze mit ***a, an*** *oder* ***the****!*

1. Sarah has ______ nose ring.

2. ______ nose ring was a real shock.

3. Simon likes going to ______ pool.

4. Did you have ______ chance to read that book?

5. Kevin rides ______ skateboard.

6. ______ blue skateboard is Kevin's.

7. I'll have ______ apple and ______ banana.

8. Has ______ post come yet?

He *dived* into the cold water and came up for air gasping. The first shock of the cold water was more than he expected. It's always best just to *dive* in, he thought, so you get used to the water. The longer it takes you to get in, the more you *suffer*. Just *dive* in.

Simon swam over to the side of the pool and *grabbed hold of* the rail. No more school for almost two months, he thought. My summer: It will be nothing but relaxing and lying in the sun, playing guitar in the morning and evenings. His thoughts then turned to Sarah, but he didn't know what to think about her – so he preferred not to think about her. He swam to the *deep end* of the pool then went underwater and swam along the bottom of the pool. He did *somersaults* and blew air out his nose until his lungs were empty, then he swam to the surface. He looked around at the crowd and decided to get out. He swam over to a ladder, climbed out of the pool and walked back to the *deckchairs*.

Übung 5: Übersetze die Verben und enträtsele das Lösungswort!

ÜBUNG 5 !

1. schwimmen ☐ _ _ _
2. springen _ ☐ _ _
3. treffen ☐ _ _ _
4. hochsteigen _ _ _ ☐ _
5. Kopfsprung machen _ _ _ ☐
6. laufen ☐ _ _

Lösung: _ _ _ _ _ _

"Do you have any *sunscreen*?"
Kevin was standing over Simon, blocking the sun.
"Yes I do," Simon said, picking up his backpack and reaching inside. "I saved this *deckchair* for you."
"Thanks," Kevin said, throwing his bag down on the chair and putting his skateboard underneath it.
Simon finally found his *sunscreen*. "Here," he said to Kevin.

"Thanks, *mate*," Kevin said, "but you're the one who needs it. You're going to be as red as a *lobster* if you don't put some on straight away."

Simon started putting on the *sunscreen*. "My mum always throws it in," he said, "but I always forget to put it on."

"So how are things going with Sarah?" Kevin asked.

"About as well as with Susie," Simon answered.

"You're *snogging* now?"

Both boys knew that the other was hopeless with girls. They liked girls and girls liked them – but something kept everything from working out. There was a simple explanation, however. Simon was shy and there was only room for one on Kevin's skateboard. The girls who interested them were simply not the type to just follow them around.

Übung 6: Setze das Gegenteil der Wörter in Klammern ein!

The two lay back on the *deckchairs* and (1. opened) __________ their eyes. They talked about music and politics and what their *fellow students* were doing during the holidays. There were (2. short) __________ silences too. After a while, they both became very hot.

"I've got to jump in," Kevin said. "Are you coming?"

"Yes, I'm (3. cold) __________ too."

They walked up to the pool. Little kids were running around and jumping in.

"Adult swim," Kevin (4. *whispered*) __________ but no one

stopped doing anything. “It was worth a try,” Kevin said and *dived* into the pool.

Simon (5. led) __________ him. They hung on the side of the pool and looked around. They saw some people from school, but didn’t want to speak to them. Simon swam out to the *deep end* and Kevin followed, though he wasn’t as (6. bad) __________ a swimmer as Simon.

“What do you call that?” Simon asked, referring to Kevin’s swimming *stroke*.
“*Freestyle*.”
“That was not *freestyle*, Kev. It looked like a cross between *freestyle* and butterfly, and they don’t go together well.”
Kevin put his hands on Simon’s shoulders and *dunked* him. Being the better swimmer, though, Simon *grabbed hold of* Kevin’s hands and pulled him farther down and then swam away. Simon reached the surface first and watched as Kevin came up and breathed in deeply, before smiling at Simon.
“Are you two trying to *drown* each other?”
They looked up at a girl with brown hair. She had been a quiet girl at the beginning of school last year but had become a bit more *outgoing recently* – perhaps because she was playing saxophone in their band, The Sneakers.
“Hello Julia,” Simon said.
“Hey, Jules,” Kevin said, playfully changing her name.
“Where’s Susie?”
“Painting.”
“What’s she painting?”

"How should I know? She doesn't tell me anything."

"Are you going to stand there all day, Julia, or are you coming in?" Simon asked.

"I'll help you in," Kevin said, pulling himself up on the side of the pool and reaching for her *ankle*.

Julia stepped back, quickly *pinched* her nose shut and jumped over Kevin and into the water before he could *grab hold of* her. They swam around together and then got out of the pool. Julia followed the boys over to their *deckchairs*.

"Where's your towel?" Simon asked.

"My things are over there," she said, pointing a short distance away.

"I could bring your *deckchair* over here, if you want," Simon suggested.

"I can do it," she answered.

"No, I'll do it," he said, walking away. "This one?" he called.

Julia nodded her head to say 'yes' and Simon carried the *deckchair* back.

ÜBUNG 7 !

Übung 7: Welches Wort ist das „schwarze Schaf"? Unterstreiche das nicht in die Reihe passende Wort!

1. classroom, teacher, study, student
2. floor, room, wall, door
3. cough, swim, jump, *dive*
4. okay, good, fine, great
5. broken, sad, happy, tired
6. bicycle, skateboard, train, car
7. sunny, happy, rainy, windy
8. *freestyle*, butterfly, *dive*, *backstroke*

They spent the rest of the afternoon sitting on the *deckchairs* and cooling off in the pool, though Simon covered himself up.

“Should we go have a tea somewhere?” Simon suggested. The other two agreed, so he added, “We’ll meet you outside in fifteen minutes.”

The two boys went into the *locker room* to shower and change. As they entered, they saw a tall young man look at them and then leave the men’s *locker room*. It was Mick, one of the *lifeguards*.

“Why didn’t he say ‘hello’?” Kevin wondered aloud.

“Might be busy.”

Their *lockers* were in different parts of the lockerroom, so they talked over the lockers while they dressed.

“Doesn’t your skateboard fit in the *lockers*?” Simon asked.

“No. Besides, I don’t like to have it so far away from me.”

“You’re not going to ride it at the pool, Kev.”

“Why not? I go down stairs on my skateboard. Maybe one of these days I’ll go off the *diving board* on it when the *lifeguards* aren’t looking.”

“The low board or the high board?”

“The high board, naturally.”

ÜBUNG 8 !

Übung 8: Unterstreiche im folgenden Textabschnitt alle Verben im Simple Past!

They walked out and waited for Julia near where the *lifeguards’* office was. Here the *lifeguards* took their breaks, ate lunch, and waited to be called. They worked an hour in the sun, an hour at the door collecting *entry fees*, an hour in the sun and then got an hour off.

“Hey Simon, hey Kev.”

“Hey Mick,” Kevin said.

"How was university last year, Mick?" Simon asked.

"Don't ask. Are you thinking about going?"

"I don't know."

"Take my advice, don't! There's got to be a better way to get an education."

"Who's here from last year?"

"Just about everyone. Rob's back managing the pool and there's Annie, Lori, Bill, Chris – Mary didn't come back. She got married in June. There's a new guy, David, who took her place. He's a bit *thick*, but he's all right. You're a bit *thick*, right Dave?"

"What?" a voice from within asked.

"See? The pay is bad here, so they can't expect everyone they *hire* to be Albert Einstein. I should have taken a job waiting tables, but I'd rather hang out with *mates* in the evening than work in a restaurant."

Julia walked out and the three left for a café.

ÜBUNG 9 !

Übung 9: In diesen Sätzen sind die Wörter durcheinander gekommen. Wie lauten die Sätze richtig? Trage sie mit Satzzeichen und richtiger Groß- und Kleinschreibung ein!

1. man young simon shy is a

Simon is a shy young man.

2. hair sarah pink has

____

3. rides everywhere kevin skateboard his

____

4. hot day was it a pool at the very

____

5. running the pool crowded children was with

____

6. café do go to you want to a

____

7. come out only night at we

____

The next few days passed much the same way. A group of ten or fifteen people, a large circle of friends, met at the pool when the weather was nice. They swam, talked and lay in the sun.

One morning the following week, Simon *showed up* at the pool about *noon*, immediately jumped into the pool and then laid on the *deckchair*. He was getting a nice tan.
"You look like you've been to Ibiza," a girl's voice said.
Simon immediately sat up. "Sarah. I didn't think you'd ever come round here."
"Do you want some company?"
"Pull up a *deckchair*."
"What have you been up to?" Sarah asked, once she was settled on the *deckchair*.
"You're looking at it."
"Have you been playing guitar at all?"
"Yes," Simon answered. He had been practising but felt that the more he practised the worse he became. It wasn't a topic he wanted to discuss. "Have you been practising?" he asked her.

"Yes, but my mum always asks why I didn't take up the flute. Can you imagine me playing the flute?"
Both were happy when Kevin arrived.
"What are you doing here, Pinkie?" Kevin asked. "I thought you punk rock *chicks* were vampires – you only come out at night."
"Kev, *put a sock in it*," she answered.

ÜBUNG 10 !

Übung 10: Beantworte die Fragen zum Text!

1. How long are the summer holidays?

___

2. What month does the story begin in?

___

3. What colour is Sarah's hair?

___

4. Which two characters are best friends?

___

5. Do Sarah and Simon listen to the same music?

___

Kevin left and got a *deckchair*. He returned and they had a pleasant conversation. Simon and Sarah spoke to each other while speaking to Kevin. If only it was always so easy.
"I left my CD player in my *locker*," Sarah said and left to *retrieve* it. When she came back she put some music on that Kevin and Simon recognised as punk rock.

Sarah was playing it so loudly they could hear it *blasting* through the *headphones*.
Kevin leaned towards Sarah, pulled one of the *headphones* away from her ear and asked, "What's the difference between punk and heavy metal?"
"*Attitude*," she answered, taking her headphone from his hand and closing her eyes.

Übung 11: Welche der Erklärungen stimmt? Kreuze die richtige Lösung an!

ÜBUNG 11 !

1. Do you *fancy* a cup of tea?
   a) ☐ Do you like tea?
   b) ☐ Would you like a cup of tea?
   c) ☐ Did you have a cup of tea?

2. Talking to you is *like pulling teeth*!
   a) ☐ It is difficult to talk to you!
   b) ☐ It is painful to talk to you!
   c) ☐ It is easy to talk to you!

3. I don't think we have the same taste in music.
   a) ☐ We like different music at restaurants.
   b) ☐ We like different kinds of music.
   c) ☐ We like the same kind of music.

4. I must be off!
   a) ☐ I must be crazy!
   b) ☐ I must go now!
   c) ☐ I must be sure!

5. Pools are not exactly my thing.
   a) ☐ I don't know how to build pools.
   b) ☐ I don't really like pools.
   c) ☐ I don't know much about pools.

"The sausages are almost finished, Simon. Did you hear that several *lockers* were *burgled* at the pool?"
Simon's mum was preparing breakfast before she left for work. She had warmed up some baked beans and had set some toast out.
"No, mum. Probably someone who was bored," he answered, sitting down at the table and *grabbing a piece of toast*.
"Do you keep your *belongings* in a *locker*?"
"Of course, mum. I don't want to leave my *wallet* and things on a *deckchair* when I go for a swim."
"Where do you hide your *wallet*?"
"In my shoe."
"Nobody would ever think to look there," she said sarcastically.
"Well, what should I do?"
"*Mind* that you don't take anything *valuable* with you. Don't take much money with you – just enough for a drink or a snack. And don't forget your *sunscreen*."
"Oh, mum."
"You're *fair-skinned*, Simon. If you get too much sun at your age, you might regret it later – you might get *skin cancer* when you're my age or your grandparents' age."
"Isn't it time you were off to work?"
"Yes, I'm *running late*," she said, throwing off her *apron*. "Clean the kitchen before you go anywhere."
"You have a good day too," he said, with sarcasm in his voice.
Simon looked around the kitchen. There were plates and glasses and pots and pans *stacked* everywhere.

Übung 12: Ordne den passenden zweiten Teil jedes Wortes zu! Trage die richtige Nummer in das Kästchen ein!

ÜBUNG 12 !

1. swim-	☐ -guards
2. deck-	☐ -phones
3. sun-	☐ -suit
4. head-	☐ -style
5. skate-	☐ -chair
6. life-	☐ -screen
7. free-	☐ -board

It was early afternoon when Simon got to the pool.
"Your *mates* are already here, Simon," Mick said as he collected the *entry fee* from Simon and noted down his *locker* number.
"I heard about the *burglaries*."

"It was a real drama. Some woman had her watch stolen and some boys lost a few things – I don't know what it was, but I *reckon* it was money."

Simon changed into his swimsuit, *locked* his *belongings* in a *locker* and joined his friends.

"Where have you been?" Kevin asked. "We thought you'd be here early to collect the *deckchairs*. That's your job."

"Yeah, right. Push over; I'm going to put my *deckchair* right there."

The group of young people all pushed their *deckchairs* and towels in different directions to make space for Simon.

"Simon, *check this out*. I've got a new CD player. It's really cool! You can hear the bass as if it's right there in your fingers. It's absolutely *amazing*. It vibrates right through your body. Riding my skateboard is going to be a whole new experience."

Simon put on the new CD player and listened for a little bit, then passed it back to Kevin.

"What's wrong?" Kevin asked. "It's fabulous."

"It sounds good, but that's not my kind of music."

"That music is cool. Besides, you can't always listen to the same kind of music. There's more than Oasis or Blur or Coldplay."

ÜBUNG 13 !

Übung 13: Ordne die Buchstaben zu einem sinnvollen Wort!

Simon lay (1. kcab) ____________ on the *deckchair* and the others carried on their conversations or sunned themselves quietly. After a (2. eliwh) ________________, Simon got up to go for a (3. misw) ____________ and Kevin and a few of the others followed him.

"Did you (4. rahe) __________ about the *robbery* at the pool yesterday?" Simon (5. saked) __________ Kevin.

"No, I didn't hear anything."

"Hey, Lori, what's the (6. swen) __________ on the *robbery*?"

"Do you (7. wokn) __________ who did it?"

She was a dark-haired young woman, about nineteen years old, but seemed much older to the two boys. She looked at them through her sunglasses a moment without saying anything.
"That wasn't a trick question," Kevin said.
"How would I know who did it? All I know is that three *lockers* were broken into," Lori said, as if bored with the question.
"Did they break the *locks* on the *lockers*?" Simon asked, looking at the key to his *locker*, which was *tied around* his *wrist*.
"No," she said coolly.
"The *lockers* weren't damaged?" Kevin asked, surprised.
"Do I have to repeat myself?" she asked.
The two boys walked away.
"What's the matter with her?" Kevin wondered.
"Probably missing her boyfriend," Simon guessed.
"I hope she sees him again soon."

"Who's that over there, Simon?"
"Where?"
"Over there, at the *deep end* – those two men."
"I don't know. Looks like they're checking the chlorine and the pH levels of the water. They must be the pool *maintenance men*."
"What do you mean '*maintenance men*'?"
"Someone has to make sure the water's safe to swim in and to clean

the filters and check the water pumps. Someone has to make sure everything is functioning correctly. The sun affects the water. People jump in the water after lying in the sun, and they're covered with *sweat* and *sunscreen*. Keeping this water safe is a full-time job."

"Hmmm. Have you ever *noticed* them before?"

"Not them. Last year there were different people. That one guy's nearly two metres tall. He looks like a heavyweight boxer."

ÜBUNG 14 !

Übung 14: Bilde Sätze mit dem Komparativ!

1. bicycle/skateboard (few wheels)

A bicycle has fewer wheels than a skateboard.

2. July/April (hot)

____

3. desert/pool (dry)

____

4. children's swimsuits/men's swimsuits (small)

____

5. Chinese/English (difficult)

____

6. ice cream/water (cold)

____

7. pool/bathtub (big)

____

8. hip-hop/punk rock (funky)

____

After swimming around a bit they returned to their *deckchairs*. Sarah was there once again.
"Hello, Pinkie," Kevin sang.
"You're so original," Sarah said *scornfully*.
"Pinkie, do you want to hear my new CD player?"
"No, and if you call me 'Pinkie' one more time, I'm going to hurt you!"
Kevin leaned back in his *deckchair*, pulled the *headphones* over his head and started tapping his foot to the music.

Übung 15: Wähle das passende Wort für jeden Satz aus und unterstreiche es!

ÜBUNG 15 !

1. The sun effects/affects the water.
2. I want to hear/listen the new song.
3. They returned to there/their *deckchairs*.
4. He looks like/shines a boxer.
5. I'm covered with water/*sweat*.
6. Do you see/think they were here last year?
7. She took away/off the *headphones*.
8. We made place/space for Simon.

Later in the afternoon, the group of young people left the pool. After changing, Simon and Kevin looked into the *lifeguards'* office.
"Hey, Mick," Kevin said, "what do you know about those two maintenance guys?"

"Nothing."

"Do you know where they're from?"

"One is from Russia, but I don't know anything about the other one. What's it to you where they're from?"

"I was just wondering. Listen to my new CD player. It's got a great sound. It's the best thing on the market at the moment."

"How'd you get it, Kevin? Did you *nick* it?"

"No, I have a part-time job."

"What – skateboarding? That's not a job."

"I help one of my neighbours every morning. He's old and needs help around the house, so I do things for him."

Kevin handed the CD player *headphones* to Mick and pressed 'play'. Mick nodded his head and then looked really impressed.

"That has a really good sound," Mick said, "handing it back to Kevin. How much did it cost?"

"Over £200."

"You rich boys. I bet mummy or daddy bought that for you. Little Kevvy's birthday yesterday?"

Kevin made a questioning look at Simon.

"Let's go," Simon said.

"What's with Mick today?" Kevin asked.

"Maybe he didn't like your question about the *maintenance men*."

"I didn't mean anything by it."

ÜBUNG 16 !

Übung 16: Vervollständige die Sätze mit ***my, your, his, her, their*** *oder* ***our!***

1. Kevin really likes _____ skateboard.

2. Sarah has _____ nose pierced.

3. They like _____ chips with lots of salt.
4. I ride _____ bicycle to the pool every day.
5. The British like _____ tea!
6. "Excuse me, is that _____ towel?"
7. "We were wondering if you had seen _____ dog anywhere."
8. Sarah and I have _____ bicycles *locked* together.
9. Kevin helps one of _____ neighbours.
10. Simon and Kevin like spending _____ holidays at the pool.

The next two days it rained all over England. Rain clouds seemed to be anchored over the UK and Ireland. Simon stayed at home and practised guitar and Kevin played his bass, while the other friends read, played games, shopped, and did whatever it is that people do to pass time on holiday when they can't do what they really want to do. The *lifeguards showed up* for work both mornings, but the pool closed once it was clear that the rain was not going to stop. The *maintenance men* checked the *chlorine* and pH levels and then left.

The following day *dawned* dark but by 11 am, the sun had come out and by 1 pm Simon and some of his friends were once again at the pool. The sun had dried the *deckchairs*, although there were small *puddles* of water here and there on the poolside. By 2 pm, the temperature had gone up so high that the *puddles* of water had *evaporated* and the pool was once again crowded. The depressing atmosphere of the past two days was gone. The friends talked and played and pushed and swam and *dunked* each other. Some held hands and others flirted.

The afternoon passed in joking and laughter – and in serious conversations. For one afternoon, summer seemed like it might last forever: *eternal* summer and *eternal* youth. Sarah was not there from the group of friends, but so many other people were there that only Simon *noticed* her absence.

! ÜBUNG 17

Übung 17: Ordne den Substantiven die in Klammern stehenden Verben richtig zu! Verwende jedes Verb zweimal!
(blows, falls, shines)

1. The wind ______________.

2. The sun ______________.

3. The rain _____________.

4. Light ________________.

5. A *whistle* ____________.

6. Snow ________________.

"Anyone know what time it is?" Kevin asked.

"Ten to six," one of the young people answered.

"Oh no! I've got to get home. My mum will *have a fit*." He picked up his skateboard and left.

A few minutes later he returned, still in his swimsuit, his towel over his shoulder, looking *upset*.

"What's the matter with you?" Simon asked. "I thought you were leaving."

"Did I bring my CD player out here?"

"I don't think so," Simon answered, and then looked around on the ground. "I don't see it anywhere."

"I don't see it either. In fact, I don't remember seeing it."

"Me neither."

"Damn! I knew I didn't bring it out," Kevin said, sitting down on the *edge* of a *deckchair*, "but I hoped that I had and I had just forgotten. Someone broke into my *locker* and stole my CD player," he said quietly. "I remember laying it on my trainers and wrapping the *cord* around the *headphones* before I closed the *locker door*."

"Did you unlock your *locker* or was it already open?"

"It was *locked*. I had to use my key to open it."

"You've got to report it to the pool manager straight away," Simon said.

"That will do me a lot of good," Kevin said sarcastically.

"I know it's useless, but you have to do it just the same."

"Whoever took it is probably long gone by now. Did you *notice* those *maintenance men* today?"

"I never saw them," Julia answered, "but they have to come every day. Even when the pool isn't open they come, so I'm sure they were here today. We were just so busy having fun that we never *noticed* them."

"Damn!" Kevin said again, and walked away from the group and towards the *lifeguards'* office. Simon ran after his friend to see if he could be of any help.

"I want to speak to the manager," Kevin said, at the doorway to the office.

"What do you want with him?" Lori asked.

"Someone stole my CD player," Kevin answered.

"You should have left it in your *locker*," she said.

"It was in my *locker*," he responded.

! ÜBUNG 18

Übung 18: Welches Wort ist das „schwarze Schaf"? Unterstreiche das Wort, dessen Aussprache nicht zu den anderen Wörtern der Reihe passt!

1. cow, bow, know
2. let, ballet, get
3. speak, weak, break
4. Moscow, row (a boat), row (a fight)
5. blind, wind (weather), mind
6. wear, bear, tear (crying)
7. where, here, there

A young man of 23 walked over to them. Rob, the pool manager, was tall, had black hair and a broad nose. Simon and Kevin had seen him walking around, speaking with the *lifeguards*. He wasn't as friendly as the other *lifeguards*.

"What's up, Lori?"

"This is Kevin. He says someone stole something from his *locker*."

"Not just 'something'," Kevin said, angrily. "It was a new CD player that *cost me a fortune*."

"You shouldn't be bringing things like that to the pool," the manager answered. "You should leave really *valuable* things at home."

"What's the point of having *lockers* if people can break into them without any problem?" Kevin shouted. "If you don't call the police, I will. That CD player cost me more than £200."

Übung 19: Schreibe die Wörter in Großbuchstaben um!

! ÜBUNG 19

1. Change a letter in COOL to make a word for a place where you cool off. ________________

2. Change a letter in SWEET to make a word for what you do when you exercise. ________________

3. Change a letter in FALL to make a word that describes someone over two metres in height. ________________

4. Change a letter in COOK to make a word for something that has many words in it. ________________

5. Change a letter in PRIME to make a word that describes an action that is against the law. ________________

6. Change a letter in TELL to make a word for what you do if you work in a shop. ________________

The manager walked away and phoned the police. In a short while a tall policeman appeared and started asking the pool manager and Kevin some questions.
Together the three of them went to the *locker* where Kevin's *belongings* were still waiting for him.
"Are you sure you *locked* the door?"
"Of course. You can't take the key out of the door without *locking* it – you turn the key, pull it out and the *locker* is *locked*."
"And you're sure you brought it with you? Your expensive, new CD player isn't sitting at home somewhere just waiting for you?"
"I'm *positive*. I had my *headphones* on while riding my skateboard to the pool and I remember putting the player right there on my trainers," he added, pointing to the trainers sitting at the bottom of his *locker*.
"I'll have to write a report on this. You do know, by the way, that riding a skateboard on the street with *headphones* on is not only dangerous but illegal, don't you?"
"It's not like I'll be able to do it anymore anyway," Kevin said sadly.
The policeman asked Kevin for the *brand*, model and colour of the CD player and whether he still had the *receipt* for it.
"Yes, it's with the guarantee," he said. "I was going to send in the form for the guarantee, but the day turned out so nice that I decided to go to the pool instead."
"You know, there's little hope of getting it back," the policeman said.
"I know. But my CD player isn't the first thing that was stolen here."
"Is that right?" the policeman asked the manager.
"Several days ago, a few other things were stolen."

"What was taken?"
"A woman's watch and a couple of *wallets* were emptied. The watch was only worth about £85."
"Was it just like this – things taken from *locked lockers*?"
"I'm afraid so."
"Was a police report filed?"
"Yes – for the woman's watch. The boys each lost £20 or £25."
"Were there any *witnesses*?"
"No."
"Is there a *pass key* that works for all these *lockers*?"
"Yes, but I don't have one. I'm responsible only for the *lifeguards*, and none of us has a *pass key*."
"Who does have a *pass key*, then?"
"The *maintenance men*," Rob answered. "They have to clean the *lockers* occasionally, so they have to be able to open them and get inside."
"Do you have the names of the *maintenance men*? The constable is going to want to speak with them if this continues."
"I can get their names and phone numbers for you."
"They're foreigners," Kevin said.
"Is that right? Since when is that a crime?" the policeman asked.
"Foreigners are always committing crimes. They come over here and start breaking our laws."
"Do they?" the policeman asked. "And you haven't broken any laws?"
"Kevin, shut up," Simon said.
"I want my *blooming* CD player back," Kevin responded, furious again.
"I'm afraid the chances of that are not very good," the policeman repeated, "and *blaming* foreigners is stupid. There's no one group of people who steals. The main difference is how people steal."
"We'll see," Kevin said.

ÜBUNG 20 !

Übung 20: Beantworte die Fragen zum Text!

1. Do Simon and his friends know the *lifeguards*?

___

2. Where do the friends keep their clothes while they're at the pool?

___

3. What does Kevin always have with him?

___

4. How much did Kevin's new CD player cost?

___

5. Did the *maintenance men* work at the pool last year?

___

6. What is the pool manager's name?

___

7. Who does Kevin think stole his CD player?

___

8. How does the thief seem to have got in the *locker*?

___

The policeman had the information he needed from Kevin so Kevin and Simon left. A great day had suddenly turned sour.

"I'm going to be very late," Kevin said.

"I think once you tell your parents what happened, they'll understand."

"They don't know about the new CD player," Kevin said quietly. "My parents don't *notice* things like that. They would be very *upset* with me if they knew that I had bought another CD player. But the bass just sounded so good on it that I had to get it. And now it's gone."

"What are you going to tell your parents, then?"

"I don't know. I'll think of something. I'll probably just tell them I was at the pool. They'll be happy I was at the pool. They're more worried about girls these days."

"My mother too. Well, I'm really sorry about your CD player. I guess you won't feel like coming to the pool anymore."

"I don't really. But I want to find out who stole my player, so I'll be back tomorrow, if the weather is as nice as it was today."

Simon began the walk home, and Kevin got on his skateboard and, a little less joyfully, began the ride home. Simon watched his friend disappear into the distance. I've got to help him find out who stole his CD player, he said to himself. Even if we don't get it back, we have to stop whoever is stealing things at the pool.

Julia ran up behind Simon.

"Oh Simon," she said, "I can't believe it. Someone stole the £20 I had in my *purse*. I just can't believe it. You can't bring anything here anymore. That money was supposed to last me a week. It's only Tuesday, and my parents won't give me any money until next Sunday. What am I going to do? I can't even pay to get into the pool now."

Simon almost made a joke about Kevin paying for her, but then he thought about Kevin's trouble and kept the joke to himself.

"Are you sure your money was in your *purse*?"

"Of course, Simon. Where else am I supposed to keep it? Besides, my *purse* wasn't where I'd left it. It was *jammed* in one of my shoes."

"That's where I keep my *wallet*," Simon said quietly and quickly pulled his *wallet* out of his backpack. He opened his *wallet* and saw that his money was still there.

"Well, you're lucky, but I wouldn't leave it there anymore," Julia warned.

"I guess not."

They both shrugged their shoulders.

"Here," Simon said, handing her some money. "For tomorrow."

"I can't take your money, Simon. I'll see if I can get a little bit of money from my Dad. I'll tell him what happened."

They said goodbye. A *glorious* summer now seemed about to become a different kind of summer, a dark summer. Years from now when they looked back on this summer, the friends would only remember being *robbed*. Not exactly a pleasant memory, thought Simon.

! ÜBUNG 21

Übung 21: Welche der Erklärungen stimmt? Kreuze die richtige Lösung an!

1. "I'm *running late*."
   a) ☐ I am late.
   b) ☐ I am running slowly.

2. "*Check this out*."
   a) ☐ Put a mark on this.
   b) ☐ Look at this.

3. "Did you *nick* this?"
   a) ☐ Did you steal this?
   b) ☐ Did you touch this?

4. Sarah *showed up* at the party.
   a) ☐ Sarah looked at the party.
   b) ☐ Sarah went to the party.

5. "My mother will *have a fit*."
   a) ☐ My mother will be tired.
   b) ☐ My mother will be angry.

6. "This car *cost me a fortune*."
   a) ☐ This car was expensive.
   b) ☐ This car was cheap.

At home, Kevin *put up a brave front*. Inside, though, he was miserable and furious. He had spent money, which he had been saving for university, on something that had been stolen. I know it was those *maintenance men*, he said to himself, I'm sure of it. Even the pool manager said that they had a master key. They have easy access to everybody's *locker*. They can take anything they want any time they want.

"Hello, Pinkie," Kevin said, but not as energetically as usual.
"Hello, Skateboy," Sarah answered. "One of these days, Kevin, you're going to say the wrong thing at the wrong time."
"Get off it, Pinkie. Why do you have to be so serious all the time?"
"Why are you so miserable, Skateboy?"
"Someone stole his new CD player yesterday."
"That's terrible!"
"Well, I'm going to find out who stole it and even if I can't get it back I'm going to make sure everyone knows who stole it."
"Who do you think stole it?"
"The *maintenance men*."

"Come on, Kevin, why would they steal something from you?"
"They're foreigners. They're always stealing things."
"Come on, Kevin. That's such a stupid thing to say."
"They're going to learn that it's a stupid thing to steal from Kevin Jones."
"Okay, Skateboy. Go ahead and make a fool of yourself."

ÜBUNG 22 !

Übung 22: Setze die richtigen Präpositionen ein!
(in, to, for, from)

"Rob," Kevin said, "where are those *maintenance men* 1. ______?"

"I don't know. I didn't *hire* them."

"Well, if you didn't, then who did?"

"The city owns the pool, so someone 2. _____ the city government, I *reckon*. Why? What's it 3. ______ you where they're 4. ______?"

"I'm just curious. People 5. _____ some of those eastern European countries have a *reputation* 6. _____ stealing."

"Do you think you're some young Sherlock Holmes?"
Kevin walked away from the pool manager. He didn't like the *scorn*, and he was powerless again him. But I know they stole my player, he thought, and I'm going to *prove* it.

"Annie," Simon said to a young woman walking along the *edge* of the pool, swinging a silver *whistle* at the end of a long string, "have you heard anything about who might have stolen that woman's watch the other day?"

"No, I haven't heard anything. Hey you, quit running and pushing! I only know that it happened."

"Whoever it is probably took Kevin's CD player as well."

"That's awful," she said. "Hey, I said quit running and I meant it!"

"He thinks the *maintenance men* stole it," Simon said once she was listening to him again.

"That's absurd. They're nice guys. They've only ever been helpful to me."

"You're a woman."

"If that's the case, then why would they steal a woman's watch?" she asked, looking at the watch on her *wrist*.

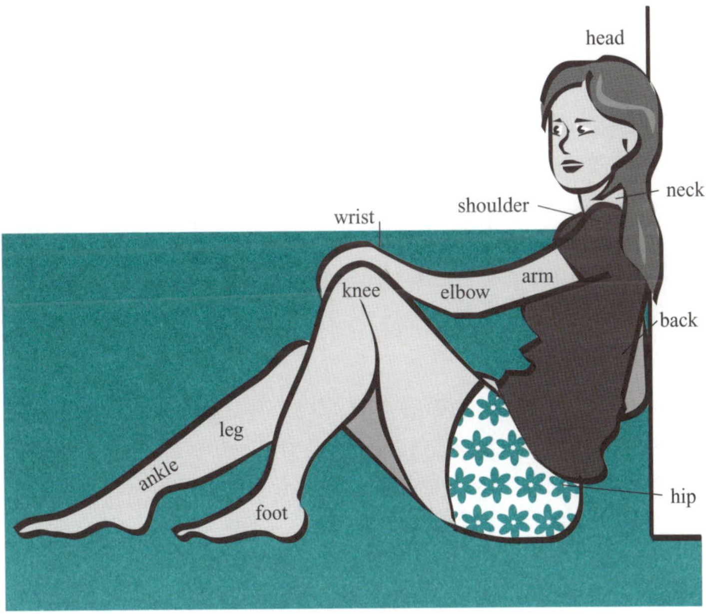

"I don't think they did it. At least I don't *assume* they did it. I just wanted to know what you knew about them."

"As I said, they've only ever been helpful to me."
"Do you know where they're from?"
"The tall blond one is Russian. I think his name is Boris. But I'd watch out, Hercule Poirot, they may not like being *accused* of being thieves."
"I'm not *accusing* anyone."

Übung 23: Trage die fehlenden Buchstaben des beschriebenen Körperteils in die Lücken ein!

1. Below your shoulders is your __ a __ k.
2. You can bend your leg using your k __ __ __.
3. Your n __ __ k holds your head up.
4. You can bend your arm using your e __ b __ w.
5. Your w __ __ st connects your hand and your arm.
6. Your __ nk __ __ connects your foot and your leg.
7. You can nod your h __ __ d to say 'yes'.

"Were you speaking to Annie earlier?" Sarah asked, walking up to Simon. Her hair was no longer pink. She had just *dyed* it a dark green.
"Yes."
"She said I was a young Miss Marple and that you were an English Hercule Poirot. What's that supposed to mean?"
"I don't know," Simon said.
"They're detectives in Agatha Christie's crime novels. You two should read more," one of their friends said.

"There they are," said Kevin.
"There 'who' are?" asked Sarah.
"The *maintenance men*, Greenie."
"I'm really going to *clout* you one of these days, Kevin."
"Simon, let's go over and see what we can hear from Vladimir and his friend."
"Who's Vladimir?"
"That's one of the *maintenance men*, the tall one."
"Annie said his name was 'Boris'," Simon corrected.
"Boris or Vladimir, it doesn't matter to me. He stole my CD player and that's the only thing that matters at the moment."
"You don't know that he stole it," Sarah said.
"Yes, I do."
They began walking in the direction of the *maintenance men*. One was *sweeping* the poolside, and the other was sitting in a white plastic chair, leaning back with his face in the sun.
"I say we just sit near them," Simon said. "I don't want to walk up to them and call them thieves."
"I'm not as stupid as all that," Kevin said. "I just want to listen to them, see if they talk about anything that might be of interest to me."
The two boys sat down very close to the two *maintenance men*. They listened for some time, staring up at the blue sky. Finally, they looked directly at each other.
"Well, it certainly isn't German," said Simon.
"And it isn't Spanish," Kevin said.
"I *reckon* it's Russian. Most of the people in Eastern Europe learned Russian, so they're probably speaking Russian."
"But they live in England, so they have to speak some English at least. I mean, they couldn't have got their jobs, could they, without speaking some English?"
"They probably speak some English," Simon agreed.

"I don't care if they speak Swahili, though. I just want either my CD player back or my £220. Nothing else matters to me."
They listened again to the men speaking. They heard one of the men say 'Boris' occasionally, so they knew Boris really was the name of one of the men. They could also hear English words – or words they thought were English – *scattered* throughout the conversation. They heard 'club' and 'table' and '*pawn*.'
"Did you hear that, Simon?"
"I don't know. What did you hear?"
"He said, '*pawn*.'"
"Are you sure it was '*pawn*'?"
"What do you think he said?"
"I'm just not sure it was '*pawn*.'"
"He said '*pawn*,'" Kevin repeated, this time more sure of himself, "and I'm sure they mean *pawnshops*. Thieves are always stealing things and then taking it to *pawnshops*. I bet they're talking about what they're doing with the *stuff* they're stealing. They might be making plans as we speak."
"They wouldn't do it here," Simon argued.
"Why not? Who speaks Russian here?"
The shorter man left for a moment and the Russian man they thought was named Boris remained. Suddenly, Boris stood, "Zoltan, Zoltan," he shouted. The boys watched as the shorter man, who had almost reached the *storage area*, turned around. "Zoltan … " The rest of what the Russian man said was in whatever language the two men were speaking, but it ended in 'cigarettes.'
"Zoltan must be his name," Simon theorised.
"Good job, Sherlock," Kevin said sarcastically.
When Zoltan returned, he was carrying a small *boombox*, an *extension cord*, and a package of cigarettes, which he threw at Boris. Boris lit a cigarette, while the other man set up the *boombox*.

“What a smelly cigarette!” Kevin said.
“I think all cigarettes are smelly. Imagine kissing someone who smokes: it must be like kissing an *ashtray*.”
“I wonder what kind of music they’re going to play,” said Kevin.
“Probably some Russian music.”

Übung 24: In diesem Gitternetz sind sechs Sprachen versteckt. Findest du sie alle?

S	P	A	N	I	S	H	G
F	A	B	T	L	E	F	E
R	D	U	T	C	H	A	R
E	N	G	L	I	S	H	M
N	F	K	M	L	D	E	A
C	P	Z	L	B	A	R	N
H	R	U	S	S	I	A	N

A look of surprise crossed Kevin’s face as he heard ‘The Payback’ by James Brown start to blast out of the *boombox*. The hard, *insistent* bass supported the song alongside the drummer.
“You look surprised,” Simon said.
“Well, aren’t you?”
“Hey, it’s James Brown.”
“I know. I love James Brown. How many times have I tried to get you interested in this CD? So much hip-hop music today *borrows* directly from James Brown or from Parliament-Funkadelic.”
“Russians listen to the Beatles and the Rolling Stones and Oasis –

why not James Brown? There's German Rap and French Rap, why not Russian Rap?"
"I'll bet they don't listen to that in Moscow."
"Don't be *thick*, Kevin. Of course they listen to that in Moscow and St. Petersburg and other cities in Russia. They may not play it in the countryside, but in the cities there must be people who listen to it."
"Well, just because they listen to music I like doesn't mean that they didn't steal my CD player."
The two boys sat there a while, listening to the music. The two men talked and laughed, and Simon and Kevin couldn't *make head or tail* of their conversation.
"They should be speaking in English," Kevin said.
"Right, and you would speak only French in France!" Simon answered.
"Okay," Kevin said. "But I think we should follow them around and see where they go."
"They probably go to other pools and work there, too."
"And steal there, too," Kevin added.
"We should see if there have been reports of thefts at other pools. But Julia lost £20 yesterday and didn't report it to the police, so police reports won't tell us everything we need to know."
"What are you two doing here?" Sarah asked, sitting down with them. "Are you listening to the music or *spying* on the *maintenance men*?"
"We aren't *spying*," Kevin said. "We're *investigating*."
Sarah listened for a moment. "It appears they're speaking a language none of us knows – probably Russian, I guess. And they're playing funk music – "
"James Brown" – Kevin put in.
" – which I expect you like."
"That may be," Kevin agreed, "but I don't like people who steal from me."

Übung 25: Sind die folgenden Aussagen richtig? Markiere mit richtig ✔ oder falsch –!

1. If a person is fit, he or she is in good physical condition. ☐
2. If you can't *make head or tail* of something, then you don't understand it. ☐
3. If there's an *entrance fee*, you get in for free. ☐
4. Kissing an *ashtray* is a pleasant experience. ☐
5. *Burglary*, *robbery* and theft have a similar meaning. ☐
6. A *thick* person is very intelligent. ☐

Sarah was angry with both boys, though more with Kevin than with Simon. This fear and hatred of foreigners is so stupid, she thought. If you hate foreigners then you don't have to try to change other things in the world, which are usually the real problem. She had *recently* been to a protest march against globalisation and against political movements that were anti-foreigner.

"Just make sure you're certain you know who *nicked* your CD player before you start *accusing* people."

"They did it all right," Kevin said.

"How do you know?" Sarah asked.

"Who else could have done it?"

"Any number of people," Sarah said.

"Come on, Greenie, they have a *pass key*. A *pass key*, Greenie. You know what a *pass key* is? It's one key that opens all *lock*. Not one *locker* but all."

"I know what a *pass key* is, Kev. *Spare me* the sarcasm."

"I think these people should be sent back to their own countries."

"So you're a skinhead, Kevin?"

"I like music made by black people. How can I be a skinhead?"

"You talk just like a skinhead, Kevin. Shame on you."

"I don't go out beating people up just because they're black or brown or look like Indians or Asians," Kevin said, defending himself.

"No, you don't. You just want to send them back 'to their own countries.' One day you're talking like that; soon you start to take action. You don't know where they were born. Plenty of people speak another language even though they were born right here in England."

"They should speak English if they live in England. And I *still* say that the *maintenance men* stole my CD player. I'll believe that until you can *prove* me wrong."

"Clearly," she said, shaking her head.

"I don't need this," Kevin said, standing up. Sarah and Simon watched Kevin walk away towards the pool and *dive* into the water.

ÜBUNG 26

Übung 26: Setze das passende Wort ein!
(stole, answer, mean, intelligent, mad, friends)

"He doesn't 1.__________ it," Simon said.

"How do you know?"

"I know him. We've been 2._________ since we were three. We've been in school together just about our whole lives. He's only 3. __________ because he lost his CD player."

"Because somebody 4.________________ his CD player," Sarah corrected.

"Right. But if the *maintenance men* didn't do it, who did?"

"That's an 5.__________question, and that's the question we have to find an 6.__________ to."

"Do you have any ideas?"
"We know that there have been at least two *robberies* here, probably more, right?"
"Right."
"So that means that it isn't someone who just came here once. It's someone who comes occasionally."
"Or regularly," Simon suggested.
"A regular," Sarah agreed. "It could be a regular."
"Someone who comes to the pool regularly. Like us."
"But we don't have access to a *pass key*."
"There are other people who come here every day or almost every day."
"We should start looking at the people who come each day and start trying to remember them. Can you think of anyone who comes regularly?"
They looked around at the people lying out on the *deckchairs*, people sitting on chairs at tables, people lying on the poolside, people running around at the side of the pool and people swimming in the pool.
"There's got to be more than a hundred people here," Simon said.
"More than two hundred on some days," Sarah added.
Kevin, wet, walked up to them.
"We should follow them," he said.
"Who?" Sarah asked.
"Who do you think?"
"Don't be *daft*," Sarah said, almost laughing at him.
"You think we should follow the *maintenance men*?" Simon asked.

"Right."

"And how should we do that?" Sarah asked. "We're just going to jump into our Rover and drive off right behind them?"

"I can follow them on my skateboard," he said.

"Your skateboard goes 40 or 50 miles per hour?"

"Downhill."

"There aren't enough hills around here," Simon said.

"Whose side are you on?" Kevin asked. "Hers or mine?"

"It's not a question of sides," Simon answered.

"It's a question of finding out who really *nicked* your CD player," Sarah declared.

! ÜBUNG 27

Übung 27: Welcher Satzteil enthält die richtige Redewendung? Kreuze die richtige Lösung an!

1. I'm right,
   a) ☐ ain't I?
   b) ☐ aren't I?

2. You know where you are,
   a) ☐ you don't?
   b) ☐ don't you?

3. She doesn't know me,
   a) ☐ does she?
   b) ☐ do she?

4. We're not late,
   a) ☐ we are?
   b) ☐ are we?

5. The movie is over,
   a) ☐ isn't it?
   b) ☐ ain't it?

6. The news is over,
   a) ☐ aren't they?
   b) ☐ isn't it?

The three looked over at Boris and Zoltan. They were still sitting and listening to the music that Kevin liked, moving their heads and their feet to the music. Not four metres away, they were the topic of a warm discussion. Suddenly, Boris looked at his watch and said something that must have been an order. Zoltan turned off the *boombox* and unplugged it. He carried it back to the *storage area* and rolled up the *extension cord* as well.
"They're leaving," Kevin said.
Boris got up and followed Zoltan into the *storage area*. A few minutes later, they walked along the side of the pool and walked out the exit.
"They're gone," Kevin said.
"Thank you for the report," Sarah said.
"Let's go over and see if we can see anything in their *storage area*. If you *noticed*, they didn't *lock* it."
"Why do you want to look in there?"
"I just want to see what we can see in there. Maybe they're storing things they steal in there."
"Don't you think they would *lock* it if there were something to hide?" Sarah asked.
"I think you're being a bit *daft* as well," Simon agreed. "You don't really expect to find your CD player sitting on a *shelf* in there, do you?"

"Maybe there's another room inside where they can store things." Kevin walked over to the *storage area* and Simon followed, mechanically.

"I really don't think this is a good idea," he said.

"You don't have to come along," Kevin reminded him.

ÜBUNG 28

Übung 28: Setze das Gegenteil der Wörter in Klammern ein!

They (1. ran) __________ to the *storage area* but could see almost (2. everything) __________ inside. The day was so (3. dark) __________ and the interior so dark that looking inside was like looking into a (4. white) __________ hole that *swallowed* all light. Kevin turned to look at the pool, saw that all the *lifeguards* were focused on the people in it and (5. slowly) __________ stepped into the *storage area*. Simon was thinking of joining him when one of the *lifeguards* called to him.

"Hey you, away from there."

"The pool's over here, *mate*," another *lifeguard* called.

"I was just wondering what's (6. out) __________ there," Simon said, walking to the pool.

Inside, the air was cool and it took Kevin's eyes a few moments to adjust to the darkness. He *stubbed his toes* a couple of times and had to bite his lip to keep from crying out.

There were hoses and plastic containers of *chlorine* as well as other equipment used to clean and maintain pools – a large underwater *vacuum cleaner* with an extension pole attached to it and soap for cleaning the pool walls along the waterline. As his eyes got used to the darkness, he moved to the back of the *storage area*. It was rather bigger than he had expected. He looked back towards the entrance to see if anyone was coming in. No one was, so he moved farther in. There was a work area, with many tools, and behind that a closed door. Kevin immediately made for the closed door. He stopped and listened to hear if anyone was coming. He heard nothing, so he put his hand on the *doorknob*, thought of his CD player to give him *courage*, and then twisted the knob. The door was *locked*. What's behind there, he wondered. What are they hiding in there?

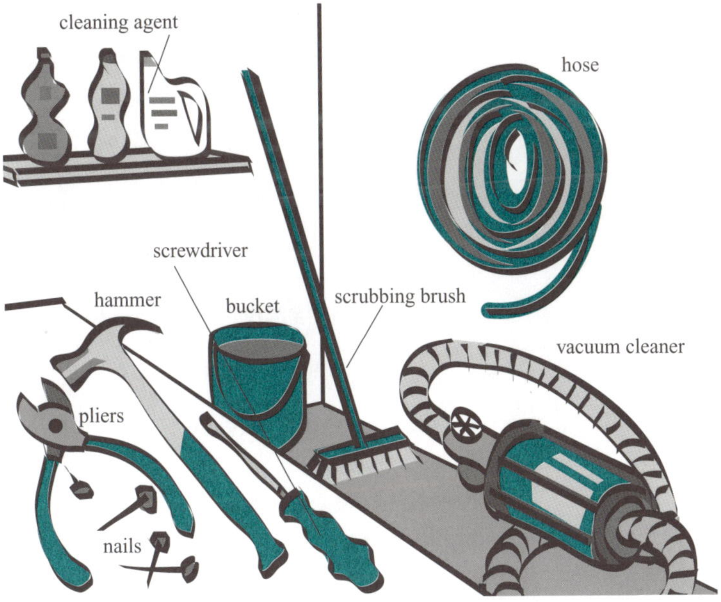

Kevin walked out quickly and went back towards the pool area. People were going about their business outside. Nobody had seen him go in, and he did not see Boris or Zoltan anywhere. It seemed that Simon had *abandoned* him. Well, Simon hadn't had a CD player stolen. He'd be thinking differently, Kevin said to himself, if he had lost something really *valuable*. Sure that his absence had gone unnoticed, he went back to the *locked* door.

ÜBUNG 29 !

Übung 29: Finde für das Wort in Klammern ein Reimwort, das in den Zusammenhang passt!

He began (1. cooking) __________ around for something to use to break in. Wooden shelves next to the *locked* (2. floor) __________ contained *screwdrivers*, hammers and many – as it turned out – *locked* drawers. Trying to pull himself up to (3. free) __________ what was on one of the shelves, Kevin discovered a (4. tree) ______________. One couldn't see it unless one was quite tall or (5. true) __________ that the key was there. He put the key to the (6. shock) __________, and it fit. Kevin opened the door and walked in. The dry smell of *chlorine* nearly knocked him out. Several large windows lit the room. A short distance away were two large, circular metal containers – two (7. carry) __________ large containers. Water was pumped from the pool to these (8. thanks) __________, passing through filters, to be cleaned. On the other side of these tanks, Kevin realised, must be the pool. To his left, along a (9. fall) __________, were more shelves, filled with an assortment of things – towels, baskets, *lane lines* for swimming competitions and the *boombox*. He didn't see his CD player, however.

"I should take their *boombox*," he said quietly, "as revenge."

"Where's Kevin?" Sarah asked.
"Yes, where is Kevin?" Julia asked, looking at Sarah.
"He'll be right back," Simon said to Julia and then leaned over and *whispered*, "He went into the *storage area*."
"And you didn't go in with your best friend?"
"I wanted to, but one of the *lifeguards* saw me so I couldn't follow him."
"Lucky you."
"What do you mean? He's my *mate*. I try to keep him from doing mad things, but he has to make his own decisions."
"Look who's coming back," Sarah said.
Simon followed her finger and saw the two *maintenance men* returning. He looked towards the *storage area*, then to the table where he and Kevin and Sarah had been sitting but saw no sign of Kevin. Kevin, he realised, was still inside looking around. Simon stood up.
"What are you going to do?" Sarah asked.
"I don't know, but if they find him, who knows what they might do?"
"They might turn him over to the police."
"Or they might do something worse."
"You don't think you could fight them, do you? The tall one would break you and Kevin in two just like matchsticks."

"No," Simon said, looking shyly at Sarah. "I know I'm no fighter, but I can't just sit here either."
"Choose your *evil*," Sarah said. They watched the two men enter the *storage area*.
Simon walked up to the pool and then towards the *storage area*. He sat down on the hot white *concrete* poolside, close enough, he thought, that he could hear if there was any sort of *punch-up*.

ÜBUNG 30

Übung 30: Vervollständige die Sätze mit ***he, his, him, she*** *oder* ***her****!*

1. Sarah spoke with Kevin but she couldn't understand ________.
2. Kevin jokes with Sarah about ________ hair.
3. The *maintenance men* are not friends of (Kevin's) ________.
4. She doesn't know what ________ can do.
5. Give (Kevin) ________ back ________ CD player!

Kevin was examining the shelves, looking for his CD player. Suddenly he heard the sound of footsteps. The *maintenance men* were returning. They seemed to be walking quickly. Did they know he was in there? The shelves in front of Kevin appeared to contain lost and found items from years past. Everything on the shelves was useless or cheap or needed to be repaired. There were also a few tools, but most of the items on the shelves were just rubbish.
Hearing the voices, Kevin looked around for a place to hide. The door to the pump room was open and the key was still in the door. It was too late for him to run out of the room and out of the storage *area*. He looked at the tanks and ran towards them. Running around behind the farthest one, he discovered a ladder on it. He immedi-

ately climbed to the top. Carefully he looked over the *edge*, expecting to see a head at any moment. He was not long in waiting. Boris came in and *glanced* around the room. He walked in and started looking around. "Hello?" he called. Kevin could only hear the sound of Boris' shoes. Suddenly he *noticed* the footsteps were coming right for him. He heard the sound of a ring against the ladder. Oh, no! If he comes up here, I'll knock the ladder down and run out, Kevin thought. Then he saw the ladder go up in the air and against the wall. Boris wasn't coming up. Though Kevin couldn't understand a word, it was clear that he was *telling* Zoltan *off*. Zoltan followed him in. Zoltan, stretching out his arms and raising his shoulders, must have been saying, "I don't know why the door is open." Boris looked around carefully one more time, looked along the floor, but never looked up and saw Kevin. Satisfied that the room was empty, Zoltan walked out first and Boris followed him.

Übung 31: Setze die Verben in der richtigen Zeitform ein!

The door (1. to close) ______________ and Kevin (2. to hear) ______________ the *lock* go into place. He waited what seemed an eternity before he (3. to come) ______________ down from the tank, which was harder since the ladder was gone, and walked over to the door. He (4. to press) ______________ his ear to the door but couldn't (5. to hear) ______________ anything. He (6. to put) ______________ his hand to the *doorknob* and (7. to try) ______________ to turn it, but it would not turn. When he (8. to look) ______________ at the knob to see if it was possible to unlock it from within, he saw there was simply another keyhole on the inside. He (9. to feel) __________ along each of the shelves next to the door but did not find a key.

"Now you (10. to get) ___________ yourself into it," he said.

Simon watched the two men leave the pool area again. He watched the *lifeguards* as well. For whatever reason, he felt that they were watching him. Sarah walked up and sat down next to him.
"Are you going to go in?" she asked.
"Yes, if Kev doesn't come out soon."
"Did you hear anything?"
"I could hear one of them shouting, but I never heard Kevin's voice, so I *assume* he wasn't shouting at Kevin."
"That's good."
Simon and Sarah waited a while, but Kevin still did not reappear.
"I've got to get in," Simon said, "and see if anything happened."
Sarah stood and jumped in the water. She swam towards the middle of the pool and came up behind a student a year ahead of them. Robin Parker was known as being tough, although Sarah claimed he was only a talker and that he wasn't tough at all. She climbed on his back and *dunked* him. He came up and started yelling at her. At that moment, with all the *lifeguards* looking at Sarah and Robin Parker, Simon slipped into the *storage area*.
"Kevin," he called quietly. "Kevin."
He wandered around but did not see any signs of Kevin. Finally, he *noticed* the door. Simon walked to the door, tried the *doorknob*, but discovered that the door was *locked*. He tried the door several times and then gave up. What's in there? he wondered. He turned around several times, looking around, but also listening for the return of

Boris and Zoltan. There must be some other way out of here, he said to himself. He turned to the door, one more time, and tried the handle one last time. It still didn't turn. What did you expect? he asked himself. As he started to walk away he heard a voice behind the door.

"Simon? Is that you, Simon?" The voice was quiet: almost too quiet for someone on the other side of the door to hear it.

"Yes, it's me. Is that you, Kevin?"

"Of course it is," Kevin answered.

"Well, the door is *locked*," Simon said.

"I know it is," Kevin answered, frustration in his voice.

"What do you want me to do, then?"

"Do you see the shelves on your right?"

"Yes."

"Can you reach the top *shelf*? The key should be lying there."

Simon reached his hand up but felt only dirt and dust. "I don't feel it," he said to Kevin.

"Quick," Kevin said, "you have to find it before they come back."

Simon kept trying to find the key. He moved his hand around a bit more and felt the cold metal key on the *shelf*. "I've got it," he said to Kevin.

"Quickly, now," Kevin said.

In a moment he had the door open and Kevin *bounded* out of the room.

"What's in there?" Simon asked, starting to walk in the room.

"It's the pump room," Kevin answered.

Simon *glanced* in, but Kevin pulled him back. He closed the door and removed the key and put it back on the *shelf*. The two boys walked back quickly towards the entrance, listening for the *maintenance men* the whole way. Kevin watched from inside until he saw an opportunity – the *lifeguards* were rotating stations – and said,

"Now, Simon," and pulled him out by the shoulder. Outside, the light was blinding. Kevin ran towards the pool and jumped into the water. Following his lead, Simon ran behind him and *dived* into the water. When they came up for air, the boys looked around at the *lifeguards* to see if their actions had been *noticed* but no one seemed to be paying them any special attention.

ÜBUNG 32 !

Übung 32: Finde im folgenden Textabschnitt die vier Adjektive und unterstreiche sie!

"Did you find anything?" Simon asked.
"Not really. There are dirty shelves filled with things people have lost over the years, but nothing they've lost *recently* – and nothing that looked worth stealing. I'm sure that if they wanted to they could find plenty of good hiding places in that *storage area*. And the pump room would be a perfect place to keep things safe and secure. They don't have the best hiding place for the key, but I discovered it purely by accident."

"So, did you find what you were looking for?" Sarah asked as the two boys returned to their *deckchairs*.
Kevin didn't answer, so Simon did, "Not really."
"Not yet," Kevin corrected.
"You think they have your CD player somewhere in there?" Sarah asked.
"They might. They might have other things as well."
"Isn't that the policeman from yesterday?" Simon was pointing across the pool towards the *lifeguards'* office.
"It *blooming* well is," Kevin said and walked off in the policeman's direction.

"You'd better go with him, Simon," Sarah *advised*. "You never know what he might say to the policeman."

Simon ran to catch up with his friend.

"Have you interviewed the *maintenance men*?" Kevin was asking just as Simon *approached*.

"Are you still talking about them?" the policeman asked.

"Well, of course."

"No, I haven't spoken to them. What do you think they're going to say? – Naturally, we stole the CD player? Do you really expect that?"

"I don't know what I expect them to say, but I expect someone to ask them questions."

"Look, I called the person who *hired* them and they have to go through a complete *background check* so I think they're okay. In any case, I have no reason to think they're not."

"I'll bet it was all fake – their *papers*. How can they be okay and have stolen my CD player?"

"Have there been any thefts at the other pools?" Simon asked before the policeman could answer Kevin's question.

"No, the thefts have all been here."

"So what are you doing here? Are you here to do some work or just to look at the girls in bikinis?"

"Okay, Kev," Simon said, *grabbing hold of* Kevin's arm, "I think it's time to go."

At that moment, Rob, the pool manager, appeared. He walked over to the policeman. "She's right in here," he said, directing the policeman into the *lifeguards'* office.

Kevin followed, pulling Simon with him, but waited just outside the door.

"Someone stole £70 from me," a *weeping* young woman said.

"You had it in your *locker*?"

"Yes."

"Why did you bring so much money with you?"

"I was planning on going out this evening, after swimming. I guess I'll just be going home now."

"Do you hear that?" Kevin asked Simon. "She lost a lot of money. I wonder when she was *robbed*. I'll bet that they were *robbing* her while I was in the *storage area* or when I was *locked* in the pump room."

"You mean the *maintenance men*? Didn't we see them leave?"

"We thought so, but we were mistaken unless they came right back."

"I suppose we could have been mistaken," Simon agreed, "but I really thought I saw them leave."

"Stop thinking so much," Kevin said. "They somehow *managed* to get into the women's changing room and steal money."

"But how did they *manage* to find her *locker* and get her money? There are hundreds of *lockers* and they found hers?"

"I don't know how they *managed* it. Perhaps it was just *dumb luck*."

"If so, I'd like some *dumb luck* right about now."

"You're not a foreigner," Kevin said.

"Don't start that again," Simon said. "I'm really sick of this anti-foreigner *attitude* of yours."

"It's not my fault that they're foreigners."

"Be reasonable, Kevin. They may be foreigners, but we don't know that they stole anything. You'd better get that into your *thick* head before you do something stupid."

"Now you're sounding like Greenie. Is she going to be the next girl you almost go out with?"

"Very funny. I suppose that would be just like you and Susie."

"Susie and I aren't together and never will be as far as I can see. And I won't be playing my new CD player anymore either."

Übung 33: Schreibe die Zahlen aus!

1. 17 ______________________________
2. 75 ______________________________
3. 2nd ______________________________
4. $^{1}/_{4}$ ______________________________
5. 1,400 ______________________________
6. 1,000,000 ______________________________
7. 25th ______________________________
8. 14 ______________________________
9. 40 ______________________________

ÜBUNG 33 !

"They're back," Sarah sang out. "Kevin! Wake up! Your criminals have returned."
Kevin opened his eyes and watched the two *maintenance men* walk over to the *storage area*. They entered and a few minutes later walked out, closing and *locking* the door.
"Do they always do that?" Kevin asked.
"I don't know," Sarah answered.
"I never *noticed* before," Simon added. "They probably do it each afternoon when they're finished for the day."
Kevin got up from the *deckchair*, slipped on his flip-flops and walked quickly to the pool entrance. The *lifeguard* there stamped his hand and he walked outside. He looked to his left and right – and saw the two *maintenance men* walking down the street. He followed them a short distance. They stopped next to a rather old green van. Kevin watched them drive away slowly.

ÜBUNG 34 !

Übung 34: Unterstreiche im folgenden Textabschnitt die Synonyme für die Wörter in Klammern!
(1. find out, 2. go behind, 3. believed, 4. pinched, 5. softly, 6. nice)

"So, what did you learn?" Simon asked.
"I know what kind of car they drive. It's a green van. It moves slowly. Between that and all the stop signs around town, I should be able to follow it on my skateboard."
"You're dreaming," Simon said.
"You're *daft*, you are," Sarah laughed, leaning forward to look at Kevin. "You don't really think you can follow a car on your skateboard, do you? I thought we talked you out of that yesterday."
"You can't talk me out of anything, Greenie. They stole my CD player and I'm going to *prove* it – one way or another."
"You have the right to make a fool of yourself, I *reckon*," Sarah said, lying back. "And apparently I can't talk you out of that either."
"You'll see," Kevin said quietly. "I have nothing against foreigners until they steal something from me."
Kevin walked away from his friends and up to the pool. A blond *lifeguard* stood near him. It was Chris.
"What do you know about the *maintenance men*?"
"They're new here. They worked somewhere else before coming here."
That's helpful, Kevin thought.
"They have several jobs," she added. I think they fill *vending machines* and I don't know what else they do. They always seem to be off to one place or another."
"Are they friendly?"
"Yes. To me and Lori and Annie. I think they're friendly to all the *lifeguards*, really. Why?"
"No reason. Well, actually, I just can't remember who did it last year."
"I don't remember either."

"So, are you coming to the pool tomorrow?" Simon asked Sarah.
"Probably. Something interesting is going on, and I don't want to miss out on it."
They stood looking at each other silently.
Kevin's right, Simon thought, she'll just be another woman I almost date.
Simon doesn't have enough *courage*, Sarah said to herself. He stands on the *edge* waiting to be pushed. Kevin may be wrong about a lot of things, but at least he has the drive to do something.
"How are you getting home? Are your parents picking you up?"
"I don't have a mobile phone, so my parents wouldn't know when to pick me up."
"Why don't you get a mobile phone then?"
"Because they aren't – "
"Let me guess," Simon interrupted, " – they aren't punk rock."
"Exactly."
"That's rather silly, isn't it?"
"I don't want my parents to be able to call me at any time."
"Good point. So, how are you getting home?"
"I'm walking."
"Would you like some company?" Simon asked, his face turning red in the process.
"Sure. But it'll be a long walk for you. You live in the other direction."

Übung 35: Wähle das passende Wort für jeden Satz aus und unterstreiche es!

1. Sarah likes/wants to go to the pool tomorrow.
2. They like their/there pool.

3. Someone has stole/stolen money.
4. I become/get money from my parents.
5. Rob is Mick's chef/boss.
6. Sarah *dived*/pushed into the water.
7. Sarah doesn't have/has a mobile phone.
8. "I must be of/off."
9. Kevin lost/losed his CD player.

They started walking. At first they were quiet, but then they started talking about the series of *robberies* at the pool over the previous few days.
"Who do you think is doing it?" Simon asked. "It seems to be someone who is at the pool quite often."
"Good point," Sarah said, suddenly sounding bored of the topic.
"The problem is that we can't really tell who comes regularly and who doesn't. And even if we could, they're probably mostly people like us who would have no way of getting into the *lockers*."
"Who else comes every day?"
"I don't know. The *maintenance men*."
"And?"
"I don't know."
They kept walking in silence. "You really don't know?" Sarah asked.
"I really don't know," Simon answered.
"You can't think of anyone else who comes every day – or at least nearly every day?"
"I *give up*, Sarah. I can't read your mind."
"You don't have to read my mind, Simon. It should be obvious. It's the *lifeguards*," she said quietly.
"I suppose that was rather obvious," he admitted.
"It was just *staring you in the face*."

Actually, Simon thought, Kevin was wrong. She won't even be someone I almost dated.
"If it is one of the *lifeguards*," Simon said after a while, "then which one?"
"I don't know. But when you pay your *entrance fee*, you have to sign in and your *locker* number is written down next to your name so whoever takes your money that day is probably the one who would know if you had something to steal."
"When did you *figure all this out*?"
"This morning. When I signed in and watched Lori write the *locker* number next to my name."
Simon smiled at Sarah.
"So, I'm not Miss Marple."
"And I'm not Hercule Poirot."

Übung 36: Welche der Erklärungen stimmt? Kreuze die richtige Lösung an!

ÜBUNG 36 !

1. This music is terrible!
   a) ☐ This music is bad.
   b) ☐ This music is excellent.

2. He found out about the concert too late.
   a) ☐ He heard about the concert at 10 pm.
   b) ☐ All the tickets for the concert had already been sold when he heard about it.

3. She couldn't talk him out of ordering a pizza.
   a) ☐ She couldn't talk about anything but pizza.
   b) ☐ She tried to get him to order something else besides pizza.

4. The truth is staring you in the face!
   a) ☐ The truth is obvious.
   b) ☐ The truth is friendly.

5. Could you give me a hand?
   a) ☐ Could you help me?
   b) ☐ Could you give me money?

The next day was rainy, so no one went to the pool. Simon called Kevin to tell him what he and Sarah had discussed on their walk home.

"You think one of the *lifeguards* is breaking into the *lockers* and stealing from pool customers?"

"I don't know if I think that's what is happening," Simon answered. "I'm only saying that's one possibility we hadn't thought of. Actually, it was Sarah's idea."

"I should have known. Well, I don't think the chances of that being the case are very good. The *lifeguards* are all friends of ours."

"They're not really friends of ours," Simon corrected him. "You and I are friends, but we're not really friends with the *lifeguards*. We're friendly to them and they're friendly to us, but we're not really anything more than *acquaintances*."

"We went to that party at Mick's last summer," Kevin challenged.

"*Still*, we don't really know him."

"I don't care. The *maintenance men* stole my CD player and they've been stealing money from everyone else. Nothing you can say will *convince* me that I'm wrong."

"Okay," Simon said, *giving up*. "See you at the pool tomorrow, if the weather's nice."

"Actually," Kevin said quickly, "I was going to ring you up to see if you wanted to go with me to the *pawnshops* today."

Later that day, the two met and went around to many of the *pawnshops*. They saw lots of CD players but none were new and none were the model that Kevin had just bought days earlier.
"They've still got it," Kevin decided.
"Maybe it's already been sold."
"I doubt it. It would have been pretty expensive. Who shops in these places? It isn't rich people."
"So, you think they still have it?"
"They have to have it."
The two boys gave up their search of the *pawnshops* and went back to Kevin's house to listen to music.

Übung 37: Unterstreiche die vier Sätze, die inhaltlich nicht zum Text passen!

! ÜBUNG 37

The sun shone down on the sunbathers and the bathers. The *lifeguards* were covered in a thick layer of *sunscreen*. In the air was the smell of perfume. Heat rose from the poolside in waves. Everybody was drinking cold drinks or diving into the pool to cool off. Every twenty minutes, one of the *lifeguards* taking a break went around to the other *lifeguards* to let them jump into the water to cool off. Clouds crossed the sky, blocking the sun completely.
Having finished off the big bottle of water he'd brought with him, Simon walked into the *locker room* to get his money from his *wallet*. It was dry everywhere. He opened his *locker* and pulled his *wallet* from the hiding place he had made for it: attaching it to the hanger on which his shirt hung with the aid of a rubber band. He opened his *wallet* and it was empty. There was lots of money inside. I thought I had £5 there. When I paid my entry, I used pound *coins* and loose change, but I thought I still had another £5.

"Sarah, could you lend me enough money for a bottle of water?"
"Sure," she answered, reaching into a little brown leather *purse* she carried around. "Would you put some *sunscreen* on my back, Simon?"
"I could have sworn I had £5 this morning when I got here," he said while spreading the *sunscreen* all the way down her back, "but my *wallet*'s empty now."
"Who would steal just £5?" she asked, handing Simon two pound *coins*.
"I don't know."
"Is £2 enough?"
"Yeah. I'll pay you back tomorrow."
"It's only £2, Simon. You can buy me a cup of tea sometime."
"By the way, Sarah. For a punk rocker, you do seem to be getting a bit of a tan."
"It's not illegal, Simon."
"No, but it is unusual."

Kevin and Simon got out of the pool.
"I've got to go to the toilet," Simon said.
"Me too."
The two boys walked into the *locker room* silently. The giant *fan* blowing fresh air in the *locker room* washed over any sound they might have made. They had almost reached the toilets when suddenly Kevin looked to the right. A young boy was trying to open a *locker* with a *screwdriver*.
"Hey, what are you doing?" Kevin shouted and jumped at the boy.
The boy turned and backed away from the *locker*. He held the *screwdriver* up for a moment and all three froze. Suddenly, the younger boy ran towards the main entrance. Kevin looked at Simon and then ran after the young boy. Simon ran behind his friend.

"Crash!!" Simon turned the corner to the door, and there lay Kevin on the floor.
"Are you all right?" Simon shouted.
"I'm fine," Kevin said, getting to his feet.
"What happened?"
"I hit my head on the door," he said quickly, then opened the door and ran out.
"What's going on?" shouted Annie.
The two boys ran by without answering. Out on the pavement, they looked in both directions, but the boy was gone. They turned around and looked back at the pool entrance, looked left and right again and then stopped.
"Goodness!" Kevin said. "We should have got him. How did he get away?"
"Little kids are sometimes faster than they look."
Annie walked outside to them. "What's going on?" she asked again.
"We caught that boy breaking into a *locker*," Kevin shouted.
"Don't shout at me," she answered.
"I'm sorry," Kevin said. "I haven't been myself lately."
"I'll say," Simon agreed.
"Do you think that boy stole all those things?" Julia asked.
"I don't know," Kevin answered. "I'm not going to *give up* on Boris just yet. I've got something planned for tonight."

Übung 38: Setze die richtigen Präpositionen ein!
(to, on, in, of)

ÜBUNG 38 !

Kevin had dressed and was waiting with his friends. He watched as the tall, blond maintenance man *locked* the *storage area*. Today, only Boris was working. Kevin followed him out 1. _____ the pool area with his skateboard under his arm and all his *belongings* 2. _____ his shoulder 3. _____ his backpack.

"Wish me luck," he said 4. _____ the gang as he walked away.

"You're going to need luck," Sarah said, "keeping up with him and keeping out 5. _____ trouble."

"I have a plan," Kevin said *confidently*, and walked away quickly.

"He's going 6. _____ get himself into trouble," Sarah *predicted*.

"I can't help him," Simon said. "I can't follow him 7. _____ his skateboard, and he didn't *let me in on* his plan."

"He's 8. _____ his own. He's a big boy."

Kevin followed Boris to the van. Earlier he had looked to see where the van was parked, and it was still parked in almost the same place. Clearly, they drove to different pools around the city or had some other business that *required* a vehicle. Kevin put his skateboard down, got on it and slowly skated around, waiting for the right moment. As Boris closed the door to the van, Kevin quickly skated over to the back of the van, *squatted*, and grabbed the handle of the back door.

I hope I don't see any police, he thought. He had done this three or four, maybe five times. One time he had held onto the back of a friend's car, but usually he had ridden on the back of a car driven by someone he didn't know. People always told stories of *mates* who had been badly hurt or even killed doing what Kevin liked to call 'road surfing' – but he had no other way of keeping up with Boris.

It was 5.30 pm and he wanted to see where Boris went after work. Kevin didn't know what he expected to learn, but he felt he had nothing to lose. Suddenly loud music began to *pulse* from the van. It was someone playing a cover version of a Sly and the Family Stone song.

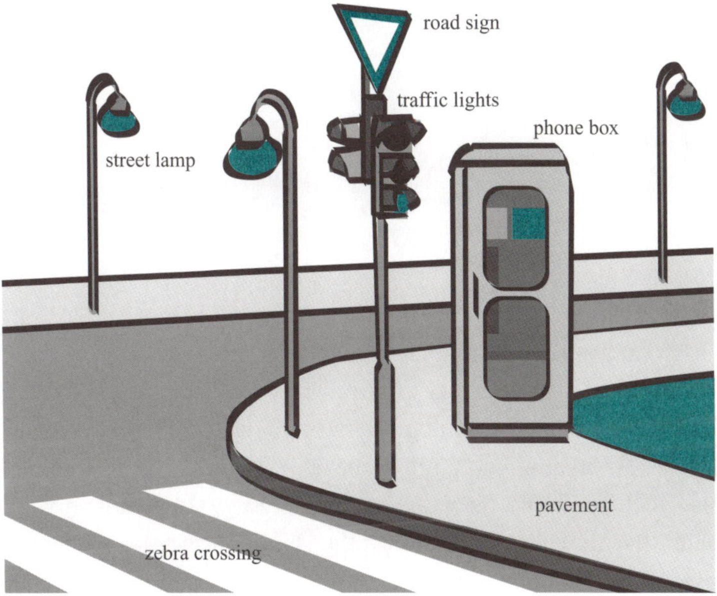

The van pulled out onto the road and picked up speed slowly. It was easy for Kevin to hold on and stay out of sight of the driver. Kevin watched houses and terraced houses and shops pass by. People on the pavement shouted to the driver that someone was on the back of his van, but because of the music Boris never heard. Drivers behind the van leaned their heads out of their windows to shout at Kevin, but he simply ignored them.

"Are you trying to kill yourself?" someone yelled at him.

Yes, of course, he wanted to yell back. Instead, he said nothing, for fear of making Boris *aware* of him.

ÜBUNG 39

Übung 39: Welche Gegenteile gehören zusammen? Trage die richtige Nummer in das Kästchen ein!

1. tall	☐ dry
2. difficult	☐ narrow
3. large	☐ safe
4. wide	☐ tiny
5. sweaty	☐ short
6. dangerous	☐ simple

Everything was going fine. Kevin saw the left-hand indicator light go on, so he was prepared to turn. Boris suddenly hit the brakes, however, when an oncoming car ran through a red light. Luckily, Kevin was holding on tightly to the door handle, so he was able to stay with the van. His skateboard, however, went flying forward under the van and straight down the street – also through the red light.

"You idiot!" Boris yelled at the driver, and then made his left turn. Kevin dropped safely from the back of the van and ran to collect his skateboard. Once he had it, he ran back to the street to follow the van. Far in the distance he spotted the vehicle sitting at a light that had just turned green. Kevin pushed the skateboard as hard as he could along the side of the road. Passing drivers yelled, but he ignored them. He was focused on one thing: the green van. Try as he might, it was slowly moving out of view, even though there were stop signs about every fifty metres and cars had to wait their turn going through the crossroads. Kevin's hair was wet, his face was covered with *sweat* and his shirt was beginning to *stick* to his skin. He kept going straight ahead and at each crossroads looked in both directions for the green van. Finally, he saw it parked in front of a nightclub, The *Prawn*.

That's not a very promising name for a club, he thought. Then he realised it was familiar and that he had heard older people talking about the club. It was a hangout for fans of hip-hop music. He was too young to get in the club, however. No doorman would let him in unless he was *outrageously* dressed. It's just six o'clock now, he thought. I bet I can get in without any problem.

Übung 40: Unterstreiche die zehn Wörter, die falsch geschrieben sind, und verbessere sie!

ÜBUNG 40

Kevin tryed the door and it opened. He walked into the cool darknesse and stood just inside the club. After a moment, he moved a little farther in and saw a large dance flur. It was dark to. Behind the dance floor was a smell stage and there stood Boris. On stage with Boris was a large sound systum with a set of speakers. Boris put on a vinyl LP and stood listening a moment, nodding his hed to the music. Kevin didn't recognise the sing, but he liked the music.

"More bass," someone shouted.

"Okay," Boris answurd, and began turning knobs.

Kevin looked for the person who had spoken to Boris. A short distance from the dance floor was a bar he hadn't *noticed*. There was a young man with dreadlocks standing in frunt of the bar.

"More!" the young man shouted again.
"That's all there is!" Boris shouted back.
"The club's not open."
Kevin turned to face Zoltan.
"It doesn't open until 9 pm."
Kevin turned round and ran out of the club as fast as he could.

Kevin rang Simon later that night.
"I followed him to a club," he reported.
"That doesn't help you, does it?"
"There's an expensive sound system there. I'll bet they bought it with money they stole from people at the pool. And I'm sure they want to buy more equipment."
"*Give it up*, Kevin. You followed him to a club. People pay to get in and that's how they finance the place. Besides, we found that boy trying to break in the *locker*."
"Maybe. I don't know. Let's talk about this tomorrow. I'm too tired to think about this at the moment."

ÜBUNG 41 !

Übung 41: Bilde das Simple Past dieser Verben!

1. stand ____________________
2. take ____________________
3. rub ____________________

4. go ______________________________

5. study ______________________________

6. give ______________________________

7. steal ______________________________

8. fly ______________________________

9. drive ______________________________

10. ride ______________________________

The next day was just as hot as the previous one. The group of friends sat at a table with a large multi-coloured parasol on it for a change. The heat was heavy like a blanket.

"So you made it on the back of the van?" Sarah asked.

"Not really."

"Not really?"

Kevin explained how he had gone quite a way before Boris had suddenly braked and sent his skateboard flying straight ahead, across the crossroads and down the road.

"You were lucky," Simon said.

"I know. And it wasn't easy jumping off the van. Luckily, it's rather slow. Anyway, I *managed* to follow him or at least to find him."

"So where did you follow him to?"

"To a club called The *Prawn*."

"Oh that place," Sarah said. "That's for people who like – who like the same kind of music as you like."

"I went in and saw Boris standing behind a sound system. And he was speaking English and setting it up."

"Did he see you?"

"No. But Zoltan did. He came up behind me and *threw me out* of the club – in English, too. He told me to come back after 9 pm. I don't think he recognised me from the pool though."

"The *Prawn*," said Sarah. "What word was it you heard the other day?"

"*Pawn*," Kevin and Simon answered together.

They looked at each other.

"You don't think they were saying '*Prawn*' now do you? I know there's only one letter difference, but there's a world of difference between '*pawn*' and '*prawn*.'"

"There is," Julia agreed, "but not in how the two words sound."

"Think of it," Sarah added, "they aren't native speakers, so maybe they say the word just a little differently."

"It can't be that big a difference," Kevin said.

"Are you sure, Kevin?" Sarah asked. "Are you so sure of yourself?"
"If I didn't know better, I'd swear you were all working with them."
"But you do know better," Julia jumped in.
"You haven't *convinced* me," Kevin said *stubbornly*. "You haven't *convinced* me that they didn't steal my CD player. Not yet."
"What about the boy we saw breaking into the *locker* yesterday?" Simon asked.
"I didn't hear about that," Sarah said. "What happened?"
Kevin explained that he and Simon had seen a boy trying to break into a *locker* with a *screwdriver*. They had stopped him and then had run after him – but he had got away.
"He can't be the one," Sarah said. "Whoever is doing this has a key of some kind. A *screwdriver* would leave marks on the *lockers*."
"You're right," Simon said. "So we're back at the beginning."
"No, we're not," Kevin disagreed. "I know who did it."

Übung 42: Trage die fehlenden Buchstaben des beschriebenen Substantivs in die Lücken ein!

1. Something you carry when it rains. _ m b _ _ l _ _
2. You wear it in the pool. _ _ _ m s _ i _
3. It's cold and comes in many flavours. _ c _ c _ _ _ _
4. Drinks come in this. b _ _ t _ _
5. You dry off with this. _ o _ _ l
6. This keeps your skin from burning. _ _ n _ _ r _ _ n
7. You keep your belongings in this. _ _ c _ _ r

Later that day, Sarah leaned over Simon and *whispered* in his ear.
"The next time you walk into the *locker room*, look up at the *ceiling*."
"Why?"
"Just do it. I want to see if you think the same thing I thought when I looked up there."
Simon felt Sarah was just playing a game with him, so he didn't *rush* to the *locker room*. He wasn't interested in mysteries. If she had something to tell him, then she should tell him straight away. Only later, while he was changing his clothes, did he remember their *whispered* conversation and look up.
The *ceiling* was not a normal *plaster* one, like in his house. It was see-through. Well, see-through, he decided, was not quite the right word. You could see *pipes* and *ventilator shafts*. Below that was an iron *grate*. Between the *pipes* there was plenty of space to *crawl* around.
Simon walked around the *locker room* looking for a way to get up into the crawl space. First I should find out if the *grate* is strong enough to hold someone, he said to himself.
With some difficulty, he climbed up on top of a row of *lockers* and put his fingers through the *grating*. He pushed up and pulled down on the *grate* but could not move it. That can hold me, he thought. How do I get up there, though? He walked all over the *locker room* but saw no place in the *ceiling* where he could make his way into the crawl space.

"Bye-bye," Simon said to Mick, as he left the pool.
"Bye-bye," Mick answered. "Having a nice lazy summer?"
Something in Mick's voice made Simon think the *lifeguard* was not being entirely friendly, but Mick was probably just having a bad day.

Übung 43: Finde für die britischen Begriffe auf der linken Seite das amerikanische Gegenstück! Trage die richtige Nummer in das Kästchen ein!

1. autumn	☐ trashcan
2. biscuit	☐ sidewalk
3. dustbin	☐ gasoline
4. pavement	☐ fall
5. queue	☐ cookie
6. petrol	☐ line

Simon walked home and thought no more about the pool or the *ceiling* in the men's *locker room*. He thought no more about the money that had been stolen, the CD player or the woman's watch. Forget it, he thought. It's my summer after all. If someone stole £5 from me, then I should be happy it was only £5.

Sarah, however, was thinking that if someone was to take a more aggressive *approach*, they might actually find out who was responsible for the thefts. As far as the police were concerned, apparently, the thefts were not really worthy of investigation. They were simply isolated incidents. The pool was not a bank or a shop but items and money seemed to be disappearing left and right. It seemed like every other day they heard someone complaining that something was missing from their *locker*. If you can't change the world, she had once been told, then at least you had to try to change your part of it – whether it was your *neighbourhood*, your village or city, or your country. Perhaps, she thought, I'll just try to solve one little problem at a swimming pool.

Kevin, naturally, was still trying to *figure out* how he could *prove* that the *maintenance men* had stolen his CD player. It was eating at him – a £220 CD player was gone one day after he purchased it. You could just never tell, he thought, about people. We're all part of Western culture, but even among Europeans there are differences. The French are different from the Germans who are different from the Swiss and the Spanish. It's a shame, he thought, because under other circumstances we might have become friends. Though we're different we have music in common.

ÜBUNG 44

Übung 44: Beantworte die Fragen zum Text!

1. How does Kevin follow Boris?

___

2. Where does Kevin look for his CD player?

___

3. Who lets Kevin out of the locked room?

___

4. What kind of club does Boris work in?

___

"Did you have a look at the *ceiling* yesterday like I asked you to?" Sarah asked, while she and Simon walked up to the pool.
"Naturally," he answered, putting his toes in the water.
"What did you think?"
"'That's a nice *ceiling*'," he answered sarcastically.
Sarah looked at him, *puzzled*. What had got into him? This whole business was making everybody a little bit crazy. It had to end – and soon.

"Okay," Simon continued, "I think I understand what you're thinking. We should hide up there and wait to see who steals money."

"Right."

"The only problem is that whoever is stealing from the *lockers* does not steal every day. We could spend a day or days up there waiting for someone to steal something. We'd be like monkeys who live in trees, hanging around, waiting for who-knows-what."

"Okay," Sarah admitted, "that's a weakness to the plan."

"I'd call that a serious weakness," Simon added.

"Well, if you're so clever, why don't you come up with a better idea?"

"Perhaps we should just let the police do their job."

"That's up to you. I've only become involved because you are – you and Kevin and Julia," she added quickly. "If you don't care, then I don't care. These thefts are meaningless to the police. They won't worry unless it's more than a few hundred pounds. One of these days, Kevin's going to make a mistake and go after the *maintenance men*. Do you want to keep him from doing something foolish?"

"How do we know they didn't steal it?"

"We don't know for sure that they didn't, but it does seem a bit too obvious, doesn't it? Just because they have a key doesn't mean they did it. It just may be that other people have a key."

"And we're supposed to hang around, up there in that crawl space, waiting?"

"I have a theory, Simon," Sarah said.

Just then, Kevin walked up behind them.

"What are you two lovebirds up to?"

Sarah pushed Kevin in the pool and then *dived* in after him. Simon watched for a moment, but the two were off in their own underwater world. He felt strange standing there just looking at them. He almost decided to join them, but then decided to go back to the *deckchair*.

"Where's Kevin?" asked Julia.
"He's in the pool. With Sarah."
Julia looked at Simon a moment, surprised.
"I thought you two were together."
"No," Simon said after a moment, "we're just friends."

ÜBUNG 45

Übung 45: Welches Wort ist das „schwarze Schaf"?

1. *ceiling*, floor, table, wall
2. village, town, city, *neighbourhood*
3. cup, plate, knife, chair
4. efficient, *handsome*, pretty, good-looking
5. bicycle, van, scooter, motorcycle
6. programme, favour, color, honour

"Remember what I said the other day?" Sarah and Simon were sitting at a table in the shade of an umbrella. "We were walking home and discussing who might be stealing from the *lockers*."
"Yes. You said that it might be one of the *lifeguards*. But who could it be? It can't be Rob or Mick or Lori or Annie or Bill or Chris. Last year they invited us to several of their parties. They wouldn't steal from Kevin."
"Have they invited you to any parties this year?"
"No, but that doesn't matter. Dave's the only person we don't know and he's the new guy. Last year we didn't have this problem. Maybe he's the one who's breaking into the *lockers* and stealing things."
"Simon, you're thinking just like Kevin: Dave isn't Russian; he's only new. If he's new, that's a good enough reason to make him the next *suspect*. He's also got his eyebrow pierced, that's a good enough reason, isn't it? What about Rob, does he speak to anyone?

No. Maybe he's the one breaking into the *lockers*."

"Who do you think it is?"

"I have some ideas."

"Are you going to share them?"

"No, I'm not, Simon."

"Do you mind explaining why you're going to *keep me in the dark*?"

"I just want to keep it to myself. I want to see if you come to the same *conclusions* that I have."

"I *reckon* you're telling everything to Kevin, so I'll just ask him. He's my friend, too."

"He still thinks Boris and Zoltan did it. He wants to believe they did it. He needs to believe they did it. If he stops thinking they did it, he won't know who to be mad at. Right now, he needs someone to be mad at. You should just be glad he's not mad at you."

Übung 46: Formuliere die Sätze im Passiv!

1. Boris drove the van.

The van was driven by Boris.

2. Simon did not steal the CD player.

____

3. Simon freed Kevin from the room.

____

4. Simon disappointed Sarah.

____

5. My parents drove me to the airport.

____

6. Simon and Sarah suspected one of the *lifeguards.*

____

Kevin was riding his skateboard to the pool when he saw the green van. He stopped and *glanced* inside. The passenger side door is unlocked. I'll be right back, he thought and got back on his skateboard.

"Julia, I need your help for a few minutes."

Kevin walked away from the group of friends towards the pool entrance. He was fully dressed and carrying his skateboard. Julia followed him.

"What do you want?"

"I want you to sit here and watch for Boris and Zoltan or whatever their names are."

"What are you going to do?"

"That's not important."

"You're not going to tell me? Well, okay. If I see them, what should I do?"

"Just walk to the entrance and call my name as loud as you can."

"I don't like this, Kevin."

Kevin walked away, away from the pool and out of view. He walked down the pavement until he came to the green van. He knew the chances of finding the CD player in the van were about as good as winning the lottery – and one always heard that one had a better chance of *getting struck by lightning* than winning the lottery. So, he thought, I have a better chance of *getting struck by lightning* than finding my CD player in this van, but I have to look.

Übung 47: Setze das Gegenteil der Wörter in Klammern ein!

Since the van was open, getting inside wouldn't be (1. easy) d_____________. With any luck, he would only be in the van for (2. more) l__________ than a minute or two. Kevin (3. slowly) q__________ looked in both directions. He could almost see the table at the pool entrance where he paid his *entry fee* each day. (4. Unfortunately) L____________, the *lifeguards* couldn't see him. He knew, however, that many other people could: the van was parked in front of a store, so he had to be fast. Setting his skateboard on its side, he opened the door and climbed inside. He started looking around in the front before moving to the back of the van. He moved tools and other equipment lying about, in order to see if the CD player were there. He looked (5. nowhere) e__________, but it was clear that his CD player was not in the van. He pulled a box out from under the back seat but it contained nothing of interest so he (6. opened) s__________ it. He looked (7. away from) t__________ the pool but saw no sign of Julia. Suddenly, there was a knock on the van window. Kevin turned to look and there was a man of about forty, with a thick black moustache, looking at him.

"Get out!" The man reached into the van, unlocked the side door, opened it and pulled Kevin out.

Kevin was so surprised he didn't even *struggle*. The man pulled him into his shop, which was dark and sold books and magazines and drinks and ice cream. "What were you doing?" Kevin didn't answer. "Say nothing, that's fine." The man pulled out a mobile phone and dialled a number. Kevin was starting to wake up, to think about to how to get out of this mess when he heard the man say, "Hello, Boris, this is Ray. I found someone going through your van."

At that very moment, Kevin pushed the man, who fell over a box and landed on the floor. In a second, Kevin was outside, and on the skateboard that still lay in front of the van. He pushed off away from the swimming pool. He went around the corner as fast as he could. I can't keep going straight on this road, he thought, it'll be too easy for him to follow me. So he turned at the next corner and made a big circle so that he came back to the pool from the other side. Before he got to the pool, though, he put his skateboard under his backpack. He saw Boris speaking to Ray for just a moment as he entered the pool. They were looking in the van, though, so they didn't see him.

"Thanks, Julia," he said.

"What were you doing?"

"Nothing."

"Don't tell me 'nothing'. You're sweating. You've done something."

"Sorry, but that's my answer."

"Well, the next time you want my help you know my answer, too." Julia walked off angrily.

"Hey, Mick."

"Hey, Kevin. How's it going?"

"All right, and you?"

"Same thing, different day."

Simon and Sarah were in the pool, hanging onto the side, talking of the coming school year. They still had nearly three weeks before school started again, but the summer was passing fast.

"Julia's really *cheesed off* with Kevin," Sarah reported. "He asked her to watch for the *maintenance men* while he did something outside the pool."

"I'll bet he broke into their van," Simon *whispered*.

"That would be foolish."

"That doesn't mean he didn't do it."

"It means he probably did do it. If he's breaking into cars now, Simon, he's getting really serious. I think it's time we took action – we'd better do something before he gets himself into trouble."

"What can we do?"

"We need to get into that crawl space and watch what happens."

"I thought we already agreed that that wasn't the best plan. We could be waiting up there until Christmas."

"I don't think so," Sarah said *confidently*. "I think there's some intelligence behind all this."

"What are you thinking?"

"Do you have a digital camera?"

"Me? Of course not. My Dad has one, but I don't."

"Could you use it?"

"I'd probably have to ask, but I *reckon* he'd let me. I'd have to promise to be careful and all that, but he trusts me. I think he does, anyway."

"I have one that I can use too. We also need a mobile phone."

"We can use mine, but why do we need a mobile phone?"

"To call the police. First, we take pictures of the person opening a *locker* and then going through it. Finally, we call the police. We'll let the police *do the dirty work*. That's what they're paid for."

"You finally found a use for a mobile phone."

"Well, I don't plan on calling the police very often."
"I know – the police aren't really punk rock."
"They aren't punk rock at all, Simon."

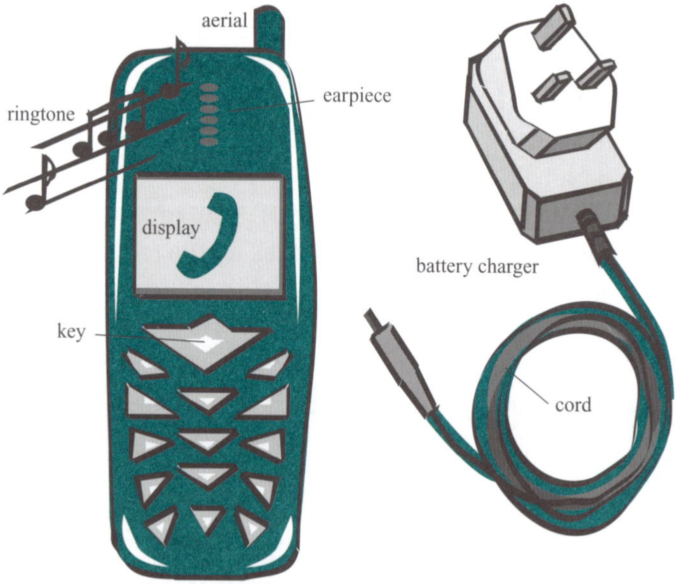

"Have you *figured out* how we can get up there? I walked all over the boys' *locker room* and couldn't find any way up."
"Then you'll just have to come over into the girls' *locker room*. On one side, there's a space where you can climb in, if you're careful. I *reckon* they left it open on the girls' side because they thought we wouldn't be climbing up there all the time. Boys are always doing something *daft*."
"I still don't want to just sit up there all day."
"We won't have to. We'll come in around *noon*."
"How does that help us?"

"They're going to steal from us."
"From us? I already lost £5. I don't want to lose more."
"You want a picture of someone stealing your money, don't you?"
"Not exactly."
"It might help the police find out who stole Kevin's CD player."
"Okay, I'll risk £10, but that's all. I'm sorry that someone stole Kevin's CD player, but life's hard."
"*You're all heart*."
"You have to be practical sometimes."
Sarah studied Simon's face a moment and then said, "I'll call you tomorrow morning so we can meet before coming to the pool."

Übung 48: Schreibe die Wörter in Großbuchstaben um!

ÜBUNG 48 !

1. Take away a letter from SUITE to make a word for what you wear at a pool. ___________
2. Change a letter from FOUR to make a word for something that has sixty minutes. ___________
3. Change a letter in JEANS to make the second word in a kind of food – baked. ___________
4. Change a letter in TRY to make a word for something people do when they're sad. ___________
5. Change a letter in BLOCK to make a word for something that tells you what time it is. ___________

6. Change a letter in HONEY to make a word for coins and notes. __________

7. Change a letter in SHORT to make a word for something you wear. __________

Four of the friends left together that day – Sarah, Julia, Simon and Kevin. As they passed the *lifeguards'* office, Dave and Chris both said "Goodbye."

"Goodbye," Simon said, a little uncomfortably.

"See you tomorrow," Sarah said.

"Not me," Dave said, "I have the day off. You'll have to put up with Mick."

"Hmmm," Sarah said.

"What are you up to tonight?" Simon asked Kevin.

"I'm going to the *Prawn*."

"Doing some *investigating*?"

"No. I'm just going to see if I can get in. Zoltan said that I could come in after 9 pm, so I'm going to see if I really can."

"Will your parents allow you out?" Julia asked.

"Of course not, but I'm not going to ask them. I'm just going to leave quietly a short time after nine o'clock. I'll tell them I'm tired after a day in the sun at the pool. They'll just be glad for a bit of peace and quiet. They're not always happy that I play bass. 'That's not a *profession*,' my father is always telling me. My mother is always asking me if we play nice songs. They'll be glad for a bit of peace, and I'll be out of the house."

"You're life sounds so tragic," Julia said. "You poor baby."

"Okay ladies," Kevin said, setting his skateboard on the ground, "I'll see you tomorrow. Simon – *behave* yourself."

"You do the same, *mate*."

Übung 49: In jedem Satz steht ein Wort an der falschen Stelle. Verschiebe es mit einem Pfeil an die richtige Stelle!

1. Kevin saw yesterday where Boris works.

2. Sarah spoke about to Simon the problem.

3. Why Kevin did go into the *storage area*?

4. Who the *deckchairs* moved?

5. Julia said, "I'll never again help you."

6. I'm about the problem thinking.

The three friends watched Kevin ride away and then each went their *separate* ways.
Sarah said something to Simon but he couldn't hear a word. When she repeated herself, he read her lips – "I'll call you tomorrow morning."

"Simon, telephone."
He walked down the stairs, rubbing his eyes.
"You need to change your boxer shorts," his mother said.
Simon picked up the telephone and said, "Hello."
"Simon, are you wearing dirty underwear?" Sarah asked.
"Mum," Simon said. "Hello, Sarah."
"What Simon?" his mother asked.
"She heard you."
"Stop *whinging*. Was that just something between you and your mother?" Sarah laughed.
"Could we get on with it?" Simon asked. "I'm tired. I was reading till late last night, so I'm not in the best *mood*."

"Okay, here's the plan. Let's meet at the Rockin' Café at half past eleven and we'll see who's on duty at the entrance."

"Who are we looking for?"

"Mick."

"Why Mick?"

"Think about it."

"What?"

"Think about it. I'll meet you in a bit, Simon. Put on something clean."

ÜBUNG 50 !

Übung 50: Setze das passende Wort ein!
(broke, desk, entrance, wallet, tomorrow, collecting, reason)

Sarah and Simon stood not far from the 1.____________ to the pool. They each had a drink in their hands, and they were looking to see who was 2. ____________ the *entry fee*. Their plan was to go in once Mick was at the 3. ____________ with the sign-in sheet.

"How much money do you have in your 4. ______________?" Sarah asked.

"£10."

Sarah *frowned* at him. "I have some money that looks real, if he only *glances* at it quickly. £20 notes. We have to give him some 5. __________ to want to *rob* you. I'm going to bring in a digital camera that my father 6. _________ last Christmas. Since the two of us will look like we have something to steal, chances are better that he'll go after one of us. If it isn't him, then we'll try someone else 7. __________."

"That's just what I was afraid of. I don't want to spend the rest of my summer up there in the *ceiling*."

"Relax, Simon."

They waited until they saw Mick take a seat behind the desk, and then they walked up to the pool entrance.

Simon pulled out his *wallet* and opened it wide. There appeared to be a lot of money in it. Simon pulled out a £5 note and paid his *entry fee*. Sarah pulled out a digital camera and took a picture of Simon.

"You shouldn't take that camera out in the sun," Simon warned. "It's not good to cook cameras."

"Don't worry. I'm not taking it out."

They signed in and went to their *lockers* and then met out in the pool area. They got their *deckchairs* and turned them around so they faced away from the pool. No one in the *lifeguards'* office would be able to see if they were there or not. "We'll be back in a little while."

Simon returned to his *locker*, got a shirt, his digital camera and his mobile phone. The previous evening, he had programmed the police phone number into this phone. He walked back to the entrance to the boys' *locker room*, which wasn't far from the front entrance. He walked out quietly, saw Mick's back and quickly ran into the girls' room. Just inside Sarah met him.

"Wait a moment," she *whispered*. "There's a woman in the toilets."

They waited silently. Finally, they heard the toilet *flush* and after that feet walking towards the pool area.

"Come, quickly," Sarah *whispered*.

Übung 51: Übersetze die Wörter und trage sie in das Kreuzworträtsel ein!

HORIZONTAL
1. sicher
5. Schließfach
6. Decke

VERTIKAL
1. Lagerraum
2. Geldbeutel
3. Geld
4. stehlen

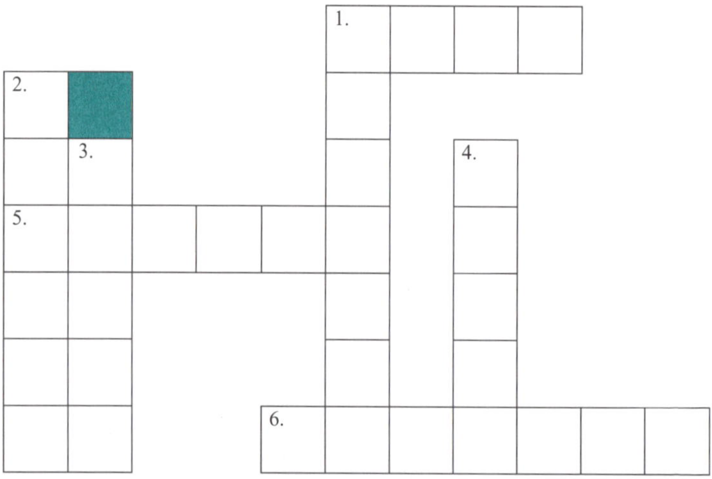

They ran to the area with the toilets and sinks.

“There it is,” she pointed. “We can get in there.”

Simon stepped on the back of the toilet, pulled himself up the wall separating the toilets and *managed* to get up into the crawl space over the *locker room*.

“Do you think it’ll support both of us?”

“Both of us?” Simon asked.

“Yes, you’re watching in the boys’ room and I’m in the girls’ room.”

"I *reckon* it will. If it doesn't, we'll be in big trouble."
Simon helped Sarah climb up, as much as he could. Both could nearly sit up in the crawl space. With Sarah leading, they *crawled* over to the wall dividing the boys' and girls' *locker room*. The wall didn't go up into the *ceiling*.
"This is comfortable," Simon said ironically.
They found that from the middle they each had a good view of their *locker room*. Each could find a comfortable position.
"I hope this holds us," Simon said.
"If one of the *lifeguards* comes in," Sarah said, "we should *crawl*, as quietly as possible, to a place where we can get good pictures. The *fans* in the *locker rooms* will hide some of the sound, but if you aren't careful they might *still* hear us."
Simon *crawled* around a bit to get used to moving about – quietly – on the *ceiling*. Then they sat together, waiting.
"Did Kevin go out last night?" Simon *whispered*.
"Yeah. He said the club is cool, even if the name is boring."

Übung 52: Welche Wörter gehören zusammen? Trage die richtige Nummer in das Kästchen ein!

ÜBUNG 52 !

1. to make	☐ a van
2. to ride	☐ a cold
3. to drive	☐ a mistake
4. to do	☐ a picture
5. to catch	☐ an idea
6. to get	☐ a promise
7. to break	☐ homework
8. to take	☐ a bike

They waited one hour and then two hours. People came in, changed from their street clothes to their swimsuits and left. Up in the crawl space, the two young people began to feel a bit warm.

"I'm not sure this was a good idea," Simon said.

"Stop whinging. Mick saw that digital camera and he thinks you have lots of money in your *wallet*. He'll be coming."

A while later, Simon looked at his watch. "It's half past two. He's not coming."

"You have to be patient, Simon. By the way, remember not to let the flash go when you take a picture. It'll give us away."

"That probably won't be a problem."

They waited.

And waited.

"Who's that?" Sarah asked.

Simon leaned forward.

"That's only Lori," he said, and leaned back.

Sarah watched the *lifeguard* walk over to the toilets and enter one of them. A minute later, she walked out and went into the *cupboard* where the *cleaners* kept their supplies. She took out a sign that warned those who wanted to come in to wait ten minutes: the *locker rooms* were being cleaned. She carried it over to the pool entrance to the *locker room*. You could not see the sign from the pool; you would only be able to see it if you tried to get in. Lori walked over to Sarah's *locker* and put a key in the *locker*. While watching the *lifeguard*, Sarah had been getting into position. She snapped a picture of the *lifeguard* at the *locker*, another of her opening the *locker*, another reaching around in the *locker*, another with the digital camera in her hand and a last one of her closing the *locker*. They watched Lori leave the *locker room*.

Sarah *crawled* back to Simon, a big smile on her face. "Can you believe it?" she almost laughed. "My plan worked."

"What do we do now?"

"Wait."

"We should call the police straight away."

"Just wait," Sarah repeated.

Lori returned shortly and put the cleaning sign back in the cleaners' *cupboard*.

When she was gone, Simon asked, "What are we waiting for?"

"Simon, there's a lot of money in your *wallet*. Let's see what happens."

"It's 2.57," Simon told her. "We can't wait till the pool closes."

"Don't worry, Simon. I really don't think we'll have to wait that long. Lots of people come around 3.30. I'm sure she'll be back before then."

ÜBUNG 53 !

Übung 53: Sind die folgenden Aussagen richtig? Markiere mit richtig ✔ oder falsch –!

1. Simon changed his mind about Boris stealing Kevin's CD player. ☐
2. Julia believes Kevin is right. ☐
3. Sarah is going to the pool because she wants to find out who is stealing things from the *lockers*. ☐
4. The *lifeguards* are friends of Simon, Kevin, Sarah and Julia. ☐
5. Simon has a plan to *figure out* who is responsible for the thefts. ☐
6. Simon has *courage*. ☐
7. Boris and Zoltan know that Kevin believes they stole the CD player. ☐
8. Lori stole Sarah's camera. ☐

Outside, among the group of friends, Simon and Sarah's absence was becoming strange.
"Where could they be?"
"They're in love," Kevin answered.
"I'm not sure about that," Julia said. "Sarah has her eyes on someone else, I think."
"I wonder what they're doing."
"Are they in the pool?"
"For more than two hours? Sarah doesn't like the pool that much."
"Maybe they're having a heart-to-heart talk."
"As I said," Julia said, "I don't think they're in love."
"It may be better to have such talks with someone you don't love."

In the *locker room*, Simon had decided he would sit up there until 3.30 – but not a moment longer. Once he had set an end-time, he was able to be patient. The two sat quietly – *whispering* occasionally, but saying nothing important or meaningful.

"There's Kevin," Simon *whispered*. They watched him walk into the *locker room*. He looked around a minute or two and then went back outside. "I wonder if he was looking for me."

"He can't think you're just hanging out in here."

Rob walked into the *locker room*. Just like Lori, he made sure the *locker room* was empty and then put the sign at the pool entrance to the *locker room*, closing it. At the same time, Simon turned on his digital camera and made sure the flash would not go off. Rob went directly to Simon's *locker*, put a key in and opened it. He quickly found Simon's *wallet*, opened it and took out the money and then closed the *locker*. He put the money in a pocket in his swimsuit. Simon took five pictures of Rob going through the *locker* and then shutting it.

Übung 54: Welche der Erklärungen stimmt? Kreuze die richtige Lösung an!

1. *Let me in on* your plan!
   a) ☐ Tell me what you're going to do.
   b) ☐ I don't want to help you.

2. Zoltan *threw him out* of the club.
   a) ☐ Zoltan had a party for him.
   b) ☐ Zoltan made him leave.

3. Shall I fetch you a towel?
   a) ☐ Shall I get your towel?
   b) ☐ Shall I take your towel?

4. He's *keeping me in the dark*.

a) ☐ I'm *locked* in a room.

b) ☐ There's something he's not telling me.

5. *You're all heart*.

a) ☐ You're a nice person. (Ironic)

b) ☐ You cry all the time.

6. Stop whinging!

a) ☐ Stop complaining!

b) ☐ Stop crying!

Sarah and Simon watched the door close behind Rob. "We should get out straight away," Simon said.
"Naturally. First, though, let's call the police."
Simon made the call and then they *crawled* over to the women's toilets. As they were making their way over, the *grating* they were on fell away from the *ceiling*. At the same time, a woman in her forties was walking into the *locker room*.
"What's going on?" she screamed.
"Quickly," Sarah *whispered*.
"Move," Simon agreed.
They *crawled* as fast as they could and were getting down onto the toilets when Annie walked in.
"What are you doing?" she demanded.
"Nothing."
"Simon!"
"Hello – er, uh."
"What were you taking pictures of?"
"We were taking pictures," Sarah said, "but it's not what you think."
"Who are you?"

"The police are on their way here," Sarah said, hiding her camera as best she could in her hand.
Rob *showed up* a moment later in the *locker room*.
"What are you doing in the women's toilets?" he asked Simon.
"It was just a *prank*," he explained, hiding his camera in the palm of his hand.
"This had better be good," Rob warned. "Come with me."

Übung 55: Setze die Verben in der richtigen Zeitform in die Lücken ein!

ÜBUNG 55 !

Simon (1. to *notice*) __________________ that Rob (2. not look) __________________ especially comfortable. Perhaps he (3. to see) __________ the camera. In any case, he (4. to hold) __________ onto Simon's arm, leading him out of the girls' *locker room*.

Sarah (5. to follow) __________ with Annie. As they walked out of the *locker room*, she hoped to see a policeman walking in. Instead, she (6. to see) __________ that Mick (7. to be) __________ once again at the desk.

Mick looked at Rob. "What (8. to go) __________ on?"

"I (9. not know) __________. But I (10. to expect) __________ to find out very soon."

Rob led the two into the *lifeguards'* office, followed by Annie. Mick closed the door behind them.

"What exactly were you doing in the girls' *locker room*?"
Sarah and Simon looked at each other but said nothing.
"They were up in the *ceiling*," Annie explained.
"Where?" Mick asked.
"In the *ceiling*. There's a crawl space up there."
"What were you doing up in the *ceiling*?"
"We weren't doing anything," Sarah said at last. "I was just showing him you could get up there."
"That's a lie," Annie said. "What's with the cameras?"
"I want the truth, Simon, and fast," Mick said.
Rob stood next to him silently.

ÜBUNG 56 !

Übung 56: Lies weiter und setze die richtigen Präpositionen in die Lücken ein!

There was a knock 1. __________ the door. Every one turned towards it.

"Open it," Rob said 2. __________ Annie.

A policeman stood 3. __________ the other side.

"How convenient," Annie said. "Officer, we found these two *crawling* around 4. __________ the *ceiling* of the girls' *locker room* – and they damaged it."

"Someone called the police," the policeman answered.

"Someone called you?" Rob asked.

"Yes," Sarah interrupted. "Simon called."

"Why?" Rob asked.

"I'll take over, if you don't mind," the policeman said.

"We have some pictures 5. __________ you," Sarah said.

"Yes," Simon said, handing his digital camera 6. __________ the police officer.

Though the pictures were a little small, he looked 7. __________ Rob and back 8. __________ the camera. Then he looked 9. __________ Sarah's pictures. After looking 10. __________ Annie, he said, "Who's this?"

"It's Lori, another of the *lifeguards*," Sarah answered.
"Please could you fetch this 'Lori'," the policeman said to Annie.
The policeman called his office and asked for another officer to come.
"What was taken?" the policeman asked Simon.
"A digital camera and some money," Simon answered.
"Money, that's hard to *prove*. Where did the money come from?"
"My *locker*," Simon said.
"Come with me," the policeman said. "You and you," he pointed at Rob and Lori who had just come in.
"Excuse me," Sarah said to the policeman and *whispered* into his ear.
"You too," the policeman said, pointing to Mick.
The three *lifeguards*, the policeman, Simon and Sarah all walked into the boys' *locker* room. Simon led them to his *locker*, opened it with the key on his *wrist*, and pulled out his *wallet*. Opening it, he saw that there was still money in the *wallet*. A £10 note was gone but a few of the fake £20 notes were still there. Simon looked at Sarah helplessly.

ÜBUNG 57 !

Übung 57: Finde für das Wort in Klammern ein Reimwort, das in den Zusammenhang passt!

"How many are (1. air) ______________?" she asked.

"Three."

"There were (2. heaven) ______________ in your wallet, weren't there?"

"So where are the (3. best) ______________?" the policeman asked.

Simon looked from the policeman to Rob and (4. track) ______________. "Right there," he said, "pointing to the bulge on the (5. wide) ______________ of Rob's swimsuit."

"What's in your pocket, (6. cheese) ______________?" the policeman asked.

"Nothing."

"(7. Wood) ______________, then open it."

Rob opened the pocket unhappily. Inside was a roll with several fake £20 notes and one real £10 note.
"Let's go back into your office," the policeman said.
As they walked back into the office, the second policeman came in. This was the policeman Simon and Sarah had seen before.
"What's going on?" Kevin called, from the other side of the *life-guards'* office.

"We found out who's been stealing things from people's *lockers*," Simon explained.
A look of surprise crossed Kevin's face.
"We're going to have a quick look around to see if we can find the digital camera," the first policeman said. He looked around the office but found nothing. "Let's see what's in your *locker*, please," the policeman said to Lori.
She opened the *locker*. The policeman found her clothes, some make-up and some *sunscreen* but no digital camera.
"If I might suggest," Sarah began, "you might want to look in Mick's *locker*. He was on duty when we paid our *entry fees* and he saw Simon's money and my digital camera.
"If you please," the policeman said to Mick.
"No," Mick answered.
"We can open it now or we can go down to the station, get permission and then come back. In either case, you're staying with me."

Übung 58: Unterstreiche im folgenden Textabschnitt die Gegenteile der vorgegebenen Wörter!
(1. running, 2. leaned forward, 3. pushed, 4. whispered, 5. speaking, 6. something, 7. smaller)

Mick stared at the policeman and then at Simon and Sarah before walking over to the *locker*. He opened it and then stood back. The policeman looked around a moment, found a sock and pulled the digital camera from it.
"Unbelievable!" Kevin shouted. "He must have my CD player!"
"That's long gone," Mick said, unable to remain silent.
Kevin turned red, but there was nothing he could do. Mick was bigger and the police were there to make sure nothing happened.

"Did you hear that?" Kevin asked at last.

"Yes."

Suddenly, Rob punched Simon in the back of the head.

"Rich boy!"

Simon quickly turned around, but a policeman came between the two.

"That's enough, you," he said to Rob. "You're in enough trouble, don't you think? Let's get them down to the station. I'll call a van."

Soon after, the two policemen led the group to the constable's office.

"Now that I think of it," Kevin began, "I remember the way Mick looked at the CD player and how he was a bit strange to us much of the time. If only I had seen that earlier."

"You decided the *maintenance men* were responsible and looked no farther," Sarah said. "You just stopped thinking."

"Okay, I was stupid. I don't dislike Russians or any group of people. I like meeting people from other countries and cultures. I was just so angry that I stopped thinking, like Sarah said."

"It's good you have friends who'll think for you when you stop thinking," Simon said. "You said just about every stupid thing someone can say, Kevin. I really couldn't believe it was you."

Sarah shook her head. "You surprised me. It was just one cliché after another about foreigners."

"But I don't think that way, Sarah. I don't – do I, Simon? Tell her."

"I told Sarah you weren't really like that, but you kept on saying the same stupid things, so it was hard to *prove* that you're an open, intelligent person."

"Okay, okay. I'm not prejudiced, though. I know it. Or maybe there's a part of myself I never knew existed before. I'm not like that, though. At least, I don't want to be like that."

Übung 59: In diesen Sätzen sind die Wörter durcheinander gekommen. Wie lauten die Sätze richtig? Trage sie mit Satzzeichen und richtiger Groß- und Kleinschreibung ein!

1. had idea a sarah great

____

2. locker hot in the were two very the room

____

3. doing ceiling what you are the in

____

4. the police was very angry with mick

____

5. kevin admit did his mistake

____

6. the rob thieves mick lori and were

____

Simon tried to call Kevin and then tried to call Sarah but neither of them was at home. He got on his bike and cycled into the city. I don't want to go to the pool, he thought. Maybe I'll go and look at some CDs. The best store for CDs was down in the city centre, so he pointed his bike in that direction. It was a pleasant ride. He had spent so much time at the pool *recently* that he had forgotten about his bicycle. He got to the store, *locked* up his bike and wandered in.

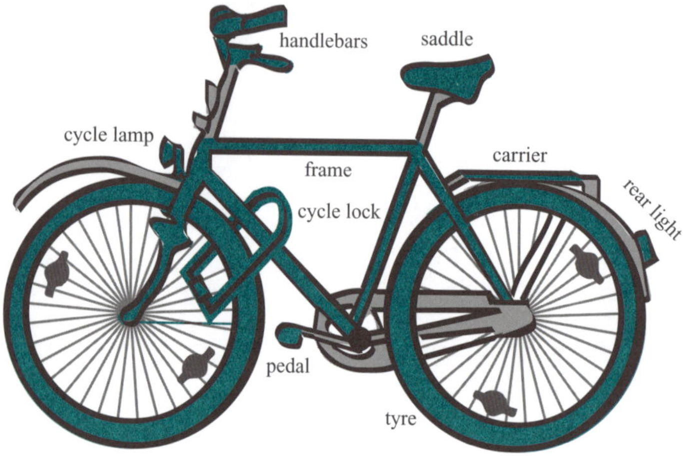

"Hey, Simon."
"Hey, Kev. Oh, hello Sarah."
"Hi, Simon."
"You just looking around?" Kevin asked. "Or are you looking for something?"
"I just thought I'd look around. I didn't know what else to do."
"I'm sick of the pool, myself," Kevin said.
"I think we all are," Sarah agreed.
"What are you up to?" Simon asked.
"We're off for some lunch. Do you want to join us?"
They looked at each other a moment. It was becoming *awkward*. Simon didn't feel like being on his own, but he knew that hanging out with Kevin and Sarah was not possible.
"No," Simon answered. He could see they were *relieved*. "I think I'm just going to cycle around. Is there any news on your CD player?"
"They found the woman's watch at Mick's house but, like Mick said, my CD player is long gone. I think they usually stole money."

"I'm sorry."
"Yeah, well, *life goes on*."

Übung 60: Ergänze die Begriffe!

ÜBUNG 60 !

1. to _ _ ke a walk
2. C _ _ c _ it out!
3. _ _ d _ my bike!
4. to _ r _ v _ a car
5. to c _ _ c _ a thief
6. C _ _ e with me!

"Simon, did you read the article in the newspaper about the pool?"
"No, mum."
"The three have been charged with stealing, but there is not much evidence of what they stole. Many people are now saying they lost money at the pool, but the police can't *prove* anything. It looks like they'll get charged with stealing the woman's watch, Kevin's CD player, the digital camera and the money found on the pool manager."
"At least that's something."
"Do you know why they were stealing from people's *lockers*?"
"No. I guess it doesn't say in the article."
"No. How did they get in?"
"They had a copy of a *pass key*. No one knows how they got it and Mick's not explaining anything."
"Where are you going?"
"Upstairs – to play guitar."
"You're not going to the pool?"
"I've had enough of the pool for one summer!"

THE END

Abschlusstest

Übung 1: Welches Wort ist das „schwarze Schaf"?

1. *lifeguard*, policeman, sunbather, swimmer
2. teacher, board, headmaster, student
3. steal, *burglary*, *daft*, theft
4. *ceiling*, house, wall, floor
5. *dive*, swim, sunbathe, jump
6. hip-hop, song, pop, punk

Übung 2: Setze die richtigen Präpositionen ein!

1. Sarah wanted __________ help Simon and Kevin.
2. Where are you __________ ? (Where were you born?)
3. Simon was worried __________ Kevin.
4. Simon flirted __________ Sarah.
5. I want to go __________ the pool today.
6. She looked __________ him while she spoke with Simon.
7. What are you up __________?

Übung 3: Ordne die Buchstaben zu einem sinnvollen Wort!

1. At a pool you can (miws) __________.

2. *Lifeguards* make sure the people in the pool are (aesf) __________.

3. According to Sarah, (basuthngni) __________ is not punk rock.

4. At the pool, you can put your belongings in a (krecol) __________.

5. To get in, you have to pay an (ytern efe) __________.

6. You dry off with a (lewto) __________ when you get out of the pool.

Übung 4: Wähle das passende Wort für jeden Satz aus und unterstreiche es!

1. Each morning I listen to/hear the radio.
2. Sarah likes/wants to go to the pool tomorrow.
3. The friends made place/space for Simon.
4. He looks like/shines a boxer.
5. Do you think/mean Sarah had a good idea?
6. I become/get £250 a week for working in a restaurant.
7. Rob is Annie, Lori and Mick's chef/boss.
8. They moved their/there *deckchairs* closer together.

Übung 5: Setze die Verben ins Simple Past!

1. Yesterday, I (to swim) __________ at the pool.

2. Simon (to run) __________ to get Kevin.

3. Sarah (to take) __________ a bus to school.

4. Lori (to answer) __________ all the questions.

5. Who (to meet) __________ you at the café last night?

6. Where (to be) __________ you on holiday last summer?

7. She (to go) __________ to Bath.

Übung 6: In diesen Sätzen sind die Wörter durcheinander gekommen. Wie lauten die Sätze richtig? Trage sie mit Satzzeichen und richtiger Groß- und Kleinschreibung ein!

1. skateboard his takes kevin everywhere almost

____

2. punk listens music sarah to rock

____

3. his simon riding bicycle enjoys

____

4. player kevin's stole who cd

____

5. russian english speaks and boris

____

6. into jumped julia water the

____

Übung 7: Welche der Erklärungen stimmt? Kreuze die richtige Lösung an!

1. Do you *fancy* seeing a film tonight?
   a) ☐ Would you like to see a movie tonight?
   b) ☐ Do you like films at the moment?

2. One can't talk with him. It's *like pulling teeth*!
   a) ☐ He doesn't say very much!
   b) ☐ It is painful to talk to you!

3. I must be off!
   a) ☐ I have to go now!
   b) ☐ I have to change my clothes!

4. Hip-hop isn't my thing.
   a) ☐ I can't play hip-hop.
   b) ☐ I don't like hip-hop.

5. He is *thick*.
   a) ☐ He is a good friend.
   b) ☐ He is not intelligent.

6. Stop whinging!
   a) ☐ Stop complaining!
   b) ☐ Stop crying!

7. It's absolutely amazing!
   a) ☐ It's fantastic!
   b) ☐ It's funny!

Übung 8: Ergänze die Begriffe!

1. To go into water feet-first is to _ u _ p.
2. When you go into water head-first you _ i _ e.
3. Paper money is also called a n _ _ e.
4. *Lifeguards* don't like it when children are _ u _ n i _ _.
5. To move on your hands and knees is to c _ a _ _.
6. When your skin is brown because of the sun you have a _ _ n t _ _.
7. The clothing you wear in a swimming pool is your s _ _ _ s _ _ t.
8. The room where you change is called a _ o _ _ _ r room.

Übung 9: Unterstreiche die zehn Wörter, die falsch geschrieben sind, und verbessere sie!

Sarah had her noise peirced and died her hair pink. Simon plaid guitar and swam. Kevin's CD player was stole, and he war angry abowt that. Julia joyned her frends at the pull.

Übung 10: Finde für das Wort in Klammern ein Reimwort, das in den Zusammenhang passt!

1. Sarah asked Kevin a question and waited for an (dancer) __________.
2. Kevin followed Boris in his van although he knew it was a big (disc) __________.
3. Simon was surprised to find that Kevin was (mocked) __________ in a room.
4. To help Simon, Sarah (junked) __________ a boy who was older than her.
5. Kevin likes to (tried) __________ his skateboard everywhere.
6. The sun can be dangerous, so don't forget your sun(mean) __________.

Übung 11: Setze die Verben in der richtigen Zeitform ein!

1. Simon (to think) __________ the summer would be quiet.
2. He (not know) __________________ how exciting it would be.
3. Kevin (to enjoy) __________ his summer until someone (to steal) __________ his CD player.
4. Simon and Kevin (to be) __________ friends since they were little boys.

5. Sarah (to have) __________ her nose pierced.

6. She (to be) __________ the first to have her nose pierced.

7. She (to go) __________ to the pool, even though she (not like) __________ the sun very much.

8. Julia (to become) __________ angry with Kevin.

9. In the story, the *lifeguards* (to collect) __________ money at the pool entrance and (to write) __________ down the locker numbers in a book.

Übung 12: Sind die folgenden Aussagen richtig? Markiere mit richtig ✔ oder falsch –!

1. It rained most of the summer. ☐
2. Simon and Kevin knew most of the *lifeguards*. ☐
3. Boris came from Bulgaria. ☐
4. Zoltan drove a blue van. ☐
5. Kevin rode his skateboard all over the city. ☐
6. It was Simon's idea to hide in the *locker rooms*. ☐
7. Kevin never suspected Zoltan of stealing the CD player. ☐
8. Sarah, Simon and Julia thought Kevin was stupid to *blame* the *maintenance men* for stealing his CD player. ☐
9. Sarah likes punk rock. ☐
10. Mick is a policeman. ☐
11. Sarah and Simon are a couple. ☐
12. Kevin is a very good swimmer. ☐
13. Sarah plays the flute. ☐

Übung 13: Welche Wörter gehören in die Lücken?
(took out, put, turned, opened, made sure, went, put, walked, closed, put, took)

Rob 1. __________ into the *locker room*. Just like Lori, he 2. __________ the *locker room* was empty and then 3. __________ the sign at the pool entrance to the *locker room*, closing it. At the same time, Simon 4. __________ on his digital camera and turned off the flash. Rob 5. __________ directly to Simon's *locker*, 6. __________ a key in and opened it. He quickly found Simon's *wallet*, 7. __________it and 8. __________ the money and then 9. __________ the *locker*. He 10. __________ the money in a pocket in his swimsuit. Simon 11. __________ five pictures of Rob going through the *locker* and then shutting it.

Übung 14: Bilde die passenden Fragen zu den vorgegebenen Sätzen!

1. Mick works as a *lifeguard*.

What does Mick do?

2. Rob is the manager at a pool.

____

3. Sarah listens to punk rock music.

____

4. They are spending their summer at the pool.

____

5. Kevin thought the *maintenance men* had stolen his CD player.

____

6. Because they had access to a *pass key*.

____

Übung 15: Wähle das passende Wort für jeden Satz aus und enträtsele das Lösungswort!

1. Kevin never _____ his CD player. □ _ _ _ _
2. Put your valuables in a _____ at the pool. _ □ _ _ _ _
3. You _____ a skateboard. □ _ _ _
4. If you like something, you _____ it. □ _ _ _ _
5. With a camera you take _____. _ □ _ _ _ _ _ _
6. A _____ works at a swimming pool. _ _ _ _ □ _ _ _ _
7. At a pool, you lie out in the _____. _ _ □
8. Please _____ a photo of me! _ _ _ □
9. You come in the pool through the _____. _ _ _ □ _

A person from another country is a _ _ _ _ _ _ _ _ _

Lösungen

Übung 1: 1. (fredom) freedom 2. (pritty) pretty 3. (noise) nose 4. (whering) wearing 5. (moar) more 6. (thay) they 7. (cupple) couple 8. (werth) worth 9. (stuppid) stupid 10. (boared) bored
Übung 2: 1. answered 2. said 3. suggested 4. set 5. skated 6. looked 7. was
Übung 3: 1. what 2. where 3. why 4. who 5. how 6. what 7. which 8. who 9. when
Übung 4: 1. a 2. The 3. the 4. a 5. a 6. The 7. an, a 8. the
Übung 5: 1. swim 2. jump 3. meet 4. climb 5. dive 6. run Lösung: summer
Übung 6: 1. closed 2. long 3. hot 4. yelled/shouted 5. followed 6. good
Übung 7: 1. study 2. room 3. cough 4. great 5. broken 6. train 7. happy 8. dive
Übung 8: 1. walked 2. waited 3. took 4. ate 5. waited 6. worked 7. got
Übung 9: 1. Simon is a shy young man. 2. Sarah has pink hair. 3. Kevin rides his skateboard everywhere. 4. It was a very hot day at the pool. 5. The pool was crowded with running children. 6. Do you want to go to a café? 7. We only come out at night.
Übung 10: 1. About 6 weeks – from the end of July until the beginning of September. 2. The story begins in July. 3. Sarah's hair is pink. 4. Simon and Kevin are best friends. 5. No, they don't.
Übung 11: 1. b 2. a 3. b 4. b 5. b
Übung 12: 1. swimsuit 2. deckchair 3. sunscreen 4. headphones 5. skateboard 6. lifeguards 7. freestyle
Übung 13: 1. back 2. while 3. swim 4. hear 5. asked 6. news 7. know
Übung 14: 1. A bicycle has fewer wheels than a skateboard. 2. July is hotter than April. 3. A desert is dryer than a pool. 4. Children's swimsuits are smaller than men's swimsuits. 5. Chinese is more difficult than English. 6. Ice cream is colder than water. 7. A pool is bigger than a bathtub. 8. Hip-hop is funkier than punk rock.
Übung 15: 1. affects 2. hear 3. their 4. looks like 5. sweat 6. think 7. off 8. space
Übung 16: 1. his 2. her 3. their 4. my 5. their 6. your 7. our 8. our 9. his 10. their
Übung 17: 1. blows 2. shines 3. falls 4. shines 5. blows 6. falls
Übung 18: 1. know 2. ballet 3. break 4. row (a fight) 5. wind (weather) 6. tear 7. here
Übung 19: 1. pool 2. sweat 3. tall 4. book 5. crime 6. sell
Übung 20: 1. Yes (at least most of them). 2. They keep them in the lockers. 3. He always has his skateboard with him. 4. He says it cost over £200. 5. No, they didn't. 6. His name is Rob. 7. He thinks (one or both of) the maintenance men took it. 8. The thief may have used a pass key.
Übung 21: 1. a 2. b 3. a 4. b 5. b 6. a

Übung 22: 1. from 2. in/from 3. to 4. from 5. from 6. for
Übung 23: 1. back 2. knee 3. neck 4. elbow 5. wrist 6. ankle 7. head
Übung 24: Spanish, Dutch, English, Russian, French, German

S	**P**	**A**	**N**	**I**	**S**	**H**	**G**
F	A	B	T	L	E	F	**E**
R	**D**	**U**	**T**	**C**	**H**	A	**R**
E	**N**	**G**	**L**	**I**	**S**	**H**	**M**
N	F	K	M	L	D	E	**A**
C	P	Z	L	B	A	R	**N**
H	**R**	**U**	**S**	**S**	**I**	**A**	**N**

Übung 25: 1. richtig 2. richtig 3. falsch 4. falsch 5. richtig 6. falsch
Übung 26: 1. mean 2. friends 3. mad 4. stole 5. intelligent 6. answer
Übung 27: 1. b 2. b 3. a 4. b 5. a 6. b
Übung 28: 1. walked 2. nothing 3. bright 4. black 5. quickly 6. in
Übung 29: 1. looking 2. door 3. see 4. key 5. knew 6. lock 7. very 8. tanks 9. wall
Übung 30: 1. him 2. her 3. his 4. she 5. him, his
Übung 31: 1. closed 2. heard 3. came 4. pressed 5. hear 6. put 7. tried 8. looked 9. felt 10. have got
Übung 32: 1. dirty 2. good 3. perfect 4. best
Übung 33: 1. seventeen 2. seventy-five 3. second 4. one quarter 5. one thousand four hundred/fourteen hundred. 6. one million 7. twenty-fifth 8. fourteen 9. forty
Übung 34: 1. learn 2. follow 3. thought 4. stole 5. quietly 6. friendly
Übung 35: 1. wants 2. their 3. stolen 4. get 5. boss 6. dived 7. have 8. off 9. lost
Übung 36: 1. a 2. b 3. b 4. a 5. a
Übung 37: 1 In the air was the smell of perfume. 2. Clouds crossed the sky, blocking the sun completely. 3. It was dry everywhere. 4. There was lots of money inside.
Übung 38: 1. of 2. on 3. in 4. to 5. of 6. to 7. on 8. on
Übung 39: 1. tall/short 2. difficult/simple 3. large/tiny 4. wide/narrow 5. sweaty/dry 6. dangerous/safe
Übung 40: 1. (tryed) tried 2. (darknesse) darkness 3. (flur) floor 4. (to) too 5. (smell) small 6. (systum) system 7. (hed) head 8. (sing) song 9. (answurd) answered 10. (frunt) front
Übung 41: 1. stood 2. took 3. rubbed 4. went 5. studied 6. gave 7. stole 8. flew 9. drove 10. rode
Übung 42: 1. umbrella 2. swimsuit 3. ice cream 4. bottle 5. towel 6. sunscreen 7. locker

Übung 43: 1. autumn/fall 2. biscuit/cookie 3. dustbin/trashcan 4. pavement/sidewalk 5. queue/line 6 petrol/gasoline

Übung 44: 1. Kevin holds onto Boris's van and rides his bicycle. 2. Kevin looks in the *storage area* at the pool. 3. Simon lets Kevin out of the locked room in the storage area. 4. Boris works in a hip-hop club.

Übung 45: 1. table 2. neighbourhood 3. chair 4. efficient 5. van 6. color

Übung 46: 1. The van was driven by Boris. 2. The CD player was not stolen by Simon. 3. Kevin was freed from the room by Simon. 4. Sarah was disappointed by Simon. 5. I was driven to the airport by my parents. 6. One of the lifeguards was suspected by Simon and Sarah.

Übung 47: 1. difficult 2. less 3. quickly 4. Luckily 5. everywhere 6. shut 7. towards

Übung 48: 1. suit 2. hour 3. beans 4. cry 5. clock 6. money 7. shirt

Übung 49: (Yesterday) Kevin saw where Boris works (yesterday). 2. Sarah spoke to Simon about the problem. 3. Why did Kevin go into the storage area? 4. Who moved the deckchairs? 5. Julia said, "I'll never help you again." 6. I'm thinking about the problem.

Übung 50: 1. entrance 2. collecting 3. desk 4. wallet 5. reason 6. broke 7. tomorrow

Übung 51: HORIZONTAL: 1. safe 5. locker 6. ceiling, VERTIKAL: 1. storage 2. wallet 3. money 4. steal

Übung 52: 1. to make a mistake 2. to ride a bike 3. to drive a van 4. to do homework 5. to catch a cold 6. to get an idea 7. to break a promise 8. to take a picture

Übung 53: 1. falsch 2. falsch 3. richtig 4. falsch 5. falsch 6. richtig 7. falsch 8. richtig

Übung 54: 1. a 2. b 3. a 4. b 5. a 6. a

Übung 55: 1. noticed 2. didn't/did not look 3. had seen 4. held 5. followed 6. saw 7. was 8. is going 9. don't/do not know 10. expect

Übung 56: 1. at 2. to 3. on 4. in 5. for 6. to 7. at 8. at 9. at 10. at

Übung 57: 1. there 2. seven 3. rest 4. back 5. side 6. please 7. Good

Übung 58: 1. walking 2. stood back 3. pulled 4. shouted 5. silent 6. nothing 7. bigger

Übung 59: 1. Sarah had a great idea. 2. The two were very hot in the locker room. 3. What are you doing in the ceiling? 4. Mick was very angry with the police. 5. Did Kevin admit his mistake? 6. Mick, Rob and Lori were the thieves.

Übung 60: 1. to take a walk 2. Check it out! 3. Ride my bike! 4. to drive a car 5. to catch a thief 6. Come with me!

Lösungen Abschlusstest

Übung 1: 1. policeman 2. board 3. daft 4. house 5. sunbathe 6. song
Übung 2: 1. to 2. from 3. about 4. with 5. to 6. at 7. to
Übung 3: 1. swim 2. safe 3. sunbathing 4. locker 5. entry fee 6. towel
Übung 4: 1. listen to 2. wants 3. space 4. looks like 5. think 6. get 7. boss 8. their
Übung 5: 1. swam 2. ran 3. took 4. answered 5. met 6. were 7. went
Übung 6: 1. Kevin takes his skateboard almost everywhere. 2. Sarah listens to punk rock music. 3. Simon enjoys riding his bicycle. 4. Who stole Kevin's CD player? 5. Boris speaks Russian and English. 6. Julia jumped into the water.
Übung 7: 1. a 2. a 3. a 4. b 5. b 6. a 7. a
Übung 8: 1. jump 2. dive 3. note 4. running 5. crawl 6. suntan 7. swimsuit 8. locker
Übung 9: 1. (noise) nose 2. (peirced) pierced 3. (died) dyed 4. (plaid) played 5. (stole) stolen 6. (war) was 7. (abowt) about 8. (joyned) joined 9. (frends) friends 10. (pull) pool
Übung 10: 1. answer 2. risk 3. locked 4. dunked 5. ride 6. screen
Übung 11: 1. thought 2. did not/didn't know 3. was enjoying, stole 4. had been friends 5. has/had 6. was 7. went, did not/didn't like 8. became 9. collected, wrote
Übung 12: 1. falsch 2. richtig 3. falsch 4. falsch 5. richtig 6. falsch 7. falsch 8. richtig 9. richtig 10. falsch 11. falsch 12. falsch 13. falsch
Übung 13: 1. walked 2. made sure 3. put 4. turned 5. went 6. put 7. opened 8. took out 9. closed 10. put 11. took
Übung 14: 1. What does Mick do? 2. Where does Rob work? 3. What kind of music does Sarah listen to? 4. Where are they spending their summer?/ What are they doing this summer? 5. Who did Kevin think had stolen his CD player? 6. Why did Kevin suspect them?/Why did Kevin think the maintenance men stole his CD player?
Übung 15: 1. found 2. locker 3. ride 4. enjoy 5. pictures 6. lifeguard 7. sun 8. take 9. entry **Lösungswort:** foreigner

Glossar

Abkürzungen im Glossar

AE	*American English*
fam	*umgangssprachlich*
sl	*slang*

to abandon	hier: im Stich lassen; verlassen; zurücklassen; aufgeben
to accuse	anklagen, beschuldigen
to advise	raten, empfehlen
amazing	fantastisch, unglaublich
ankle	Knöchel
approach	hier: Vorstoß; Nähern; Zugang
to approach	herankommen, näher kommen
appropriate	passend
apron	Schürze
ashtray	Aschenbecher
to assume	annehmen, unterstellen
attitude	Haltung
awkward	unangenehm
background check	Hintergrundüberprüfung
backstroke	Rückenschwimmen
battered	abgenutzt, ramponiert *fam*
beady eyes	glänzende Knopfaugen
to behave	sich benehmen
belongings	Eigentum, persönliche Sachen
to blame	beschuldigen
blasting *sl*	mit voller Lautstärke
blooming *sl*	verdammt *fam*
boombox *sl*	Ghettoblaster
to bound	springen
to borrow	hier: entlehnen; leihen
brand	Marke

to burgle	einbrechen
burglary	Einbruch
ceiling	Decke
Check this out!	Schau hier!
to be cheesed off *sl*	die Nase voll haben *fam*
chick *sl*	Mädel *fam*, Kleine *fam*
chlorine	Chlor
clout	Schlag
coin	Münze
conclusion	(Ab-)Schluss
concrete	Beton
confidently	sicher
to convince	überzeugen
cord	Schnur, Leitung, Kabel
to cost (cost, cost) someone a fortune	jemanden ein Vermögen kosten
courage	Mut
to crawl	hier: kriechen; krabbeln
creepy	grus(e)lig
cupboard	Schrank
daft *sl*	doof *fam*
to dawn	dämmern
deckchair	Liegestuhl
deep end	Schwimmerbecken
to dive	springen, Kopfsprung machen
diving board	Sprungbrett
to do (did, done) the dirty work	die Drecksarbeit machen *fam*
doorknob	Türgriff
to drown	ertränken
dumb luck *AE*	Glücksfall
to dunk	(ein)tunken; (ein)tauchen
to dye	färben
dyed → to dye	gefärbt
edge	Kante, Rand
elbow pads	Ellbogenschützer

entrance/entry fee	Eintrittsgeld
eternal	ewig
to evaporate	verdunsten
evil	Übel
extension cord	Verlängerungsschnur
fair-skinned	hellhäutig
fan	hier: Lüfter; Fan; Fächer
to fancy, fancied, fancied	mögen
fellow students	Mitschüler
to figure something out	etwas kapieren
to flush (a toilet)	spülen
freestyle	Freistil
to frown	finster schauen
furniture	Möbel
to give (gave, given) up	aufgeben
Give it up! *sl*	Gib's auf!
to glance	blicken, mit Blicken streifen
glorious	glorreich
to grab a piece of toast *fam*	sich ein Stück Toast schnappen *fam*
to grab hold of	festhalten
grate	Gitter, Rost
grating	Gitter
handsome	gut aussehend, attraktiv
to have (had, had) a fit	einen Wutanfall haben
headphones	Kopfhörer
to hire	einstellen
insistent	hier: schrill; beharrlich; nachdrücklich; wiederholt
to investigate	untersuchen, nachgehen
to jam (jammed, jammed)	(hinein)zwängen
to keep (kept, kept) someone in the dark	jemanden im Ungewissen lassen
kneepads	Knieschützer
lane lines	Bahnseile
to let someone in on something	jemandem Bescheid sagen

life goes on	das Leben geht weiter
lifeguard	Bademeister(in)
like pulling teeth	mühsam
lobster	Hummer
to lock	abschließen
locker	Schließfach
locker room	Umkleideraum
maintenance men	Wartungsmonteure
to make (made, made) head or tail of something	aus etwas schlau werden
to manage	hier: etwas schaffen; leiten
mate *sl*	Kumpel *fam*
mood	Stimmung
neighbourhood	Nachbarschaft
to nick *sl*	klauen
noon	Mittag
to notice	merken, bemerken
outgoing	aufgeschlossen
outrageous	abscheulich
overcrowded	überfüllt
papers	Papiere
pass key	Generalschlüssel
to pawn	verpfänden
pawnshop	Pfandhaus
to pinch	klauen
pipe	Rohr
plaster	hier: Putz; Gips; Pflaster
positive	hier: überzeugt; sicher; positiv
prank	Streich
prawn	Garnele
profession	Beruf
to prove	beweisen
puddle	Pfütze
to pulse	pulsieren, pochen
punch-up	Prügelei

purse	Geldbeutel
Put a sock in it!	Du hast jetzt Sendepause! *fam*
to put up a brave front	sich nichts anmerken lassen
puzzled	verblüfft, verwirrt
receipt	Quittung
recently	vor kurzem
to reckon	glauben, meinen
relieved	erleichtert
to require	erfordern
to retrieve	hier: holen gehen; wiedererlangen; zurückbekommen
to get (got, got) rid of	loswerden
to rob	rauben
robbery	Raub
to be (was, been) running late	spät dran sein
to rush	rasen, stürzen
to scatter	verstreuen
scorn	Hohn, Verachtung
scornfully	höhnisch, verächtlich
screwdriver	Schraubenzieher
separate	getrennt
shelf	hier: Wandbrett; Bord; Regal
to show (showed, shown) up	erscheinen, auftauchen
skin cancer	Hautkrebs
to snog, snogged, snogged *sl*	(rum)knutschen *fam*
somersaults	Saltos
spare me	verschone mich
spring cleaning	Frühjahrsputz
to spy, spied, spied	ausspionieren
to squat, squatted, squatted	hocken
to stack	aufstapeln, sammeln
to stare	starren
to stare someone in the face	jemandem deutlich vor Augen stehen
to stick, stuck, stuck	hier: ankleben; kleben; feststecken
still	hier: trotzdem; noch

storage area	Lager
stroke	hier: Schwimmstil; Schlag
to struggle	kämpfen
to get struck by lightning	vom Blitz getroffen werden
to stub (stubbed, stubbed) a toe	die Zehe anstoßen
stubbornly	stur *fam*
stuff *sl*	Zeug, Kram *fam*
to suffer	leiden
sunscreen	Sonnenschutzmittel
suntan	Sonnenbräune
to suspect	verdächtigen
to swallow	(runter)schlucken
sweat	Schweiß
to sweep	fegen, kehren
to tell (told, told) someone off	jemanden ausschimpfen
that certain something	das gewisse Etwas
thick *sl*	dumm
to throw (threw, thrown) someone out	jemanden hinauswerfen
to tie around	umbinden
unbearable	unerträglich
uncomfortable	unangenehm
upset	bestürzt
vacuum cleaner	Staubsauger
valuable	wertvoll
vending machine	Automat
ventilator shafts	Lüftungsschächte
wallet	Brieftasche
to weep, wept, wept	weinen
to whisper	flüstern
whistle	hier: Pfeife; Flöte
wrist	Handgelenk
You're all heart.	liebenswürdig (ironisch)